CLOUD COMPUTING & IT'S APPLICATION WITH PRACATICAL APPROACHES

CC & ITS APPLICATION WITH PRACTICAL APPROACH

DR. RAHUL SHARMA

To all the visionaries and innovators who have pushed the boundaries of technology, this book is dedicated to you. Your relentless pursuit of knowledge and your courage to embrace change have made the world of cloud computing possible.

To the pioneers who laid the groundwork for this transformative era, your insights and creativity continue to inspire new generations.

To the countless developers, engineers, and IT professionals who work tirelessly to harness the power of the cloud, your dedication shapes our digital landscape and empowers businesses worldwide.

And to every organization and individual striving to leverage cloud technology for growth and innovation, may this book serve as a guide on your journey to unlocking the full potential of the cloud. Together, we are building a future where technology knows no bounds.

Contents

Foreword

In the rapidly evolving landscape of technology, cloud computing stands out as a transformative force reshaping how we operate, collaborate, and innovate. This book offers a comprehensive exploration of cloud computing, demystifying its complexities and highlighting its vast potential.

As organizations increasingly migrate to the cloud, understanding its core principles becomes essential. From the benefits of scalability and cost efficiency to the challenges of security and compliance, this book provides valuable insights for both beginners and seasoned professionals. It bridges the gap between theory and practical application, ensuring readers can navigate this dynamic field with confidence.

In an era where agility and resilience are paramount, embracing cloud technologies is no longer a choice but a necessity. This book serves as a vital resource for anyone looking to leverage cloud computing to drive growth and foster innovation.

I invite you to delve into the chapters ahead, engage with the concepts presented, and envision the endless possibilities that cloud computing holds for the future. Together, let us embark on this exciting journey toward a more connected and efficient digital world.

Preface

Cloud computing has fundamentally transformed the way we approach technology, enabling unprecedented flexibility, scalability, and collaboration. As organizations across industries increasingly adopt cloud solutions, understanding the principles, applications, and implications of this technology becomes crucial.

This book aims to provide a comprehensive overview of cloud computing, catering to both newcomers and experienced professionals. We explore the foundational concepts, the various service models—Infrastructure as a Service (IaaS), Platform as a Service (PaaS), and Software as a Service (SaaS)—and the numerous applications that are reshaping how businesses operate.

Throughout the chapters, we will delve into real-world case studies, best practices, and emerging trends, offering practical insights that readers can apply in their own contexts. We also address the challenges and considerations that come with cloud adoption, from security concerns to vendor management.

Acknowledgements

Writing this book on cloud computing has been an incredible journey, and I am deeply grateful to those who supported me along the way.

First and foremost, I would like to thank my colleagues and mentors for their invaluable insights and encouragement. Your expertise and passion for technology inspired me to delve deeper into the complexities of cloud computing.

I am especially thankful to the technical teams and industry professionals who shared their experiences and case studies, enriching the content with real-world applications. Your willingness to share knowledge has been instrumental in making this book both practical and relevant.

To my family and friends, thank you for your unwavering support and patience during the writing process. Your belief in my vision kept me motivated, even during challenging times.

Lastly, a heartfelt thank you to the readers. Your curiosity and drive to learn about cloud computing are what make this endeavor worthwhile. I hope this book serves as a valuable resource in your journey toward harnessing the power of the cloud.

Prologue

In the ever-evolving digital landscape, cloud computing has emerged as a pivotal force that redefines how we interact with technology. It is not merely a technological advancement; it represents a profound shift in mindset, where the boundaries of traditional IT infrastructure are expanded, and possibilities become limitless.

This book aims to explore the multifaceted world of cloud computing and its applications, illuminating its role in driving innovation, enhancing efficiency, and fostering collaboration. As businesses and individuals increasingly turn to the cloud, understanding its intricacies becomes essential for navigating this transformative journey.

We will delve into the fundamental concepts that underpin cloud services, examine various models like IaaS, PaaS, and SaaS, and showcase real-world applications across diverse industries. Along the way, we will address critical challenges, including security, compliance, and vendor relationships, equipping you with the knowledge to make informed decisions.

As you embark on this exploration, consider how cloud computing can empower you to reimagine your strategies, improve your operations, and ultimately drive success in a rapidly changing world. Welcome to the future of technology—let's unlock its potential together.

CHAPTER ONE

About to Cloud computing

Cloud computing has revolutionized how individuals and organizations store, manage, and process data. It refers to the delivery of computing services—such as servers, storage, databases, networking, software, and analytics—over the Internet ("the cloud"). This paradigm shift allows users to access technology resources on-demand, without the need for extensive physical infrastructure.

Figure: 1.1 Cloud Computing

Key Models of Cloud Computing

- Infrastructure as a Service (IaaS): This model provides virtualized computing resources over the Internet. Users can rent virtual servers and storage, allowing them to scale resources up or down as needed. Popular IaaS providers include Amazon Web Services (AWS), Microsoft Azure, and Google Cloud Platform (GCP).
- Platform as a Service (PaaS): PaaS offers a framework for developers to build, test, and deploy applications without worrying about the underlying infrastructure. This service typically includes development tools, middleware, and database management, streamlining the application lifecycle. Notable PaaS examples are Heroku and Google App Engine.
- Software as a Service (SaaS): In this model, software applications are delivered over the Internet on a subscription basis. Users can access these applications through a web browser, eliminating the need for local installation. Examples of SaaS include Google Workspace, Microsoft 365, and Salesforce.

Benefits of Cloud Computing

- Cost Efficiency: Cloud computing reduces the need for significant capital investment in hardware and software. Businesses can operate on a pay-as-you-go model, which helps to manage costs effectively.
- Scalability: Organizations can easily scale their IT resources up or down based on demand. This flexibility is crucial for handling fluctuations in workload without the need for significant infrastructure changes.
- Accessibility and Collaboration: Cloud services can be accessed from anywhere with an Internet connection, promoting remote work and collaboration. Teams can easily share files and work together in real time, enhancing productivity.
- Security: While concerns about data security in the cloud are common, reputable cloud providers invest heavily in advanced security measures, including encryption, access controls, and regular security audits, often surpassing the capabilities of in-house IT departments.
- Disaster Recovery and Backup: Cloud computing facilitates robust disaster recovery solutions. Data stored in the cloud can be backed up and restored more easily, minimizing downtime and data loss in the event of a disaster.

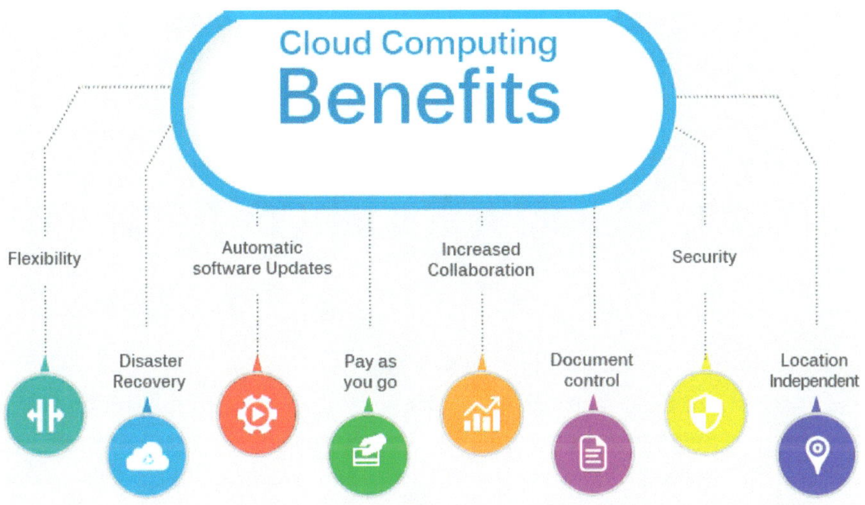

Figure: **Benefits of Cloud Computing**

Challenges and Considerations

- Despite its advantages, cloud computing is not without challenges. Concerns about data privacy, compliance with regulations, and vendor lock-in can pose significant risks. Organizations must carefully evaluate their cloud provider's security policies and ensure that they comply with relevant data protection laws.
- Additionally, while cloud services offer immense scalability, over-reliance on these services can lead to unexpected costs. Businesses need to monitor usage to avoid financial pitfalls.

Cloud computing represents a transformative shift in how technology resources are consumed and managed. By leveraging cloud services, businesses can enhance efficiency, reduce costs, and foster innovation. As technology continues to evolve, embracing cloud solutions will be essential for organizations aiming to stay competitive in an increasingly digital world.

CHAPTER TWO

Introduction Cloud computing

2.1 Introduction Cloud computing at a glance

Cloud computing represents a paradigm shift in how technology resources are delivered and consumed. Rather than relying on local servers or personal devices for storage and processing, users can access a vast array of services via the Internet—collectively known as "the cloud." This model has revolutionized everything from data management to software deployment, offering unprecedented flexibility, scalability, and efficiency.

What is Cloud Computing?

At its core, cloud computing refers to the on-demand delivery of computing services, including servers, storage, databases, networking, software, and analytics, over the Internet. This approach eliminates the need for organizations to invest heavily in physical hardware and infrastructure, enabling them to focus on their core competencies.

Cloud services are typically categorized into three main models:

- Infrastructure as a Service (IaaS): This model provides virtualized computing resources over the Internet. Organizations can rent servers and storage as needed, allowing for significant flexibility in managing IT resources.
- Platform as a Service (PaaS): PaaS offers a framework for developers to build, test, and deploy applications without dealing with the underlying infrastructure. This model streamlines the development process, providing essential tools and services.
- Software as a Service (SaaS): In this model, software applications are delivered over the Internet, allowing users to access them via a web browser without the need for local installation. This is particularly beneficial for organizations looking to simplify software management and updates.

Key Benefits
The advantages of cloud computing are numerous:

- Cost Efficiency: By adopting a pay-as-you-go model, organizations can avoid substantial upfront investments in hardware and software. This financial flexibility enables businesses to allocate resources more effectively.
- Scalability: Cloud services allow organizations to easily scale their IT resources up or down based on demand. This agility is crucial for accommodating growth or fluctuations in workload without significant disruptions.
- Accessibility: With cloud computing, users can access their data and applications from anywhere with an Internet connection. This fosters remote work and enhances collaboration among teams distributed across different locations.
- Security: While concerns about data security are prevalent, leading cloud providers invest heavily in robust security measures, including encryption, multi-factor authentication, and continuous monitoring. For many businesses, cloud security can exceed what they could achieve with in-house systems.

Challenges to Consider

- Despite its many benefits, cloud computing is not without challenges. Issues such as data privacy, compliance with regulations, and vendor lock-in require careful consideration. Organizations must conduct thorough assessments of their cloud providers to ensure they meet specific security and compliance requirements.
- Additionally, while the cloud offers remarkable scalability, organizations should monitor usage to avoid unexpected costs associated with resource over-provisioning.

Cloud computing has reshaped the technological landscape, enabling businesses to operate more efficiently and flexibly than ever before. As organizations continue to embrace cloud services, understanding its fundamentals and implications will be essential. This book aims to guide you through the intricacies of cloud computing, providing insights and practical applications that can empower you to harness its full potential.

Together, let's explore how cloud technology can drive innovation and success in today's digital age.

2.2 Historical developments

The roots of cloud computing can be traced back to the 1960s, when computer scientists like J.C.R. Licklider envisioned a future where people could access data and applications from anywhere. This concept of "Intergalactic Network" set the stage for the development of the Internet.

In the 1970s and 1980s, the emergence of virtualization technology allowed multiple operating systems to run on a single physical machine. This laid the groundwork for the resource-sharing capabilities that are fundamental to cloud computing today.

The term "cloud computing" itself began to gain traction in the late 1990s. In 1999, Salesforce.com pioneered the concept of delivering software as a service (SaaS) over the Internet, allowing users to access applications without the need for local installation. This marked a significant shift towards cloud-based services.

The early 2000s saw the introduction of Infrastructure as a Service (IaaS). Amazon Web Services (AWS) launched in 2006, providing on-demand cloud computing resources, which revolutionized the IT landscape. Companies could now scale their operations without significant upfront investment in hardware.

By the late 2000s and early 2010s, cloud computing had gained widespread acceptance across various industries. Major players like Microsoft and Google entered the market, introducing their cloud platforms—Microsoft Azure and Google Cloud Platform, respectively. This era also witnessed the rise of hybrid and multi-cloud strategies, allowing organizations to combine public and private cloud solutions.

Today, cloud computing continues to evolve with advancements in artificial intelligence, machine learning, and edge computing. The focus on security, compliance, and sustainability is reshaping how organizations approach cloud adoption, ensuring that the technology remains adaptable to future challenges.

As we look to the future, the evolution of cloud computing promises to drive further innovation, making it an integral part of modern digital transformation strategies.

2.3 Building cloud computing environments

Creating effective cloud computing environments involves several key considerations that ensure scalability, security, and efficiency. Here's a structured approach to building robust cloud infrastructures.

1. Define Objectives

Start by clearly defining your organization's objectives. Determine the specific use cases for cloud computing—whether for data storage, application hosting, or software development. Understanding these needs helps in selecting the appropriate cloud model (public, private, or hybrid).

2. Choose a Cloud Service Model

Select the right service model based on your requirements:

- Infrastructure as a Service (IaaS): Ideal for organizations needing complete control over their infrastructure, allowing for customizable virtual machines and storage.
- Platform as a Service (PaaS): Suitable for developers looking to build applications without managing the underlying hardware.
- Software as a Service (SaaS): Best for businesses that prefer ready-to-use applications without installation or maintenance.

3. Select a Cloud Provider

Research and choose a reliable cloud provider that aligns with your technical requirements and budget. Evaluate factors like:

- Performance: Look for providers with low latency and high uptime guarantees.
- Security: Ensure robust security features, including encryption and compliance with regulations like GDPR or HIPAA.
- Support: Access to responsive customer support is crucial for troubleshooting.

4. Design the Architecture

Create a scalable and flexible architecture. Consider using microservices, which allow applications to be broken down into smaller, manageable components. This modularity facilitates easier updates and scaling.

5. Implement Security Measures

Security is paramount in cloud environments. Employ multiple layers of protection, including:

- Identity and Access Management (IAM): Control user access to resources based on roles and responsibilities.

- Encryption: Protect data both in transit and at rest.
- Regular Audits: Conduct security assessments and compliance audits to identify vulnerabilities.

6. Monitor and Optimize

Once your cloud environment is operational, continuous monitoring is essential. Use analytics tools to track performance, resource usage, and costs. Regularly review and optimize your environment to enhance efficiency and reduce unnecessary expenses.

Building a successful cloud computing environment requires careful planning and execution. By defining clear objectives, selecting the right service models, ensuring robust security, and continuously optimizing, organizations can harness the full potential of cloud technology to drive innovation and efficiency.

2.4 The cloud reference model

The cloud reference model provides a structured framework for understanding the various components and services that comprise cloud computing. It helps organizations and developers visualize how different elements interact within a cloud environment, facilitating better decision-making and integration.

1. Service Models

The cloud reference model primarily categorizes cloud services into three key models:

- Infrastructure as a Service (IaaS): This foundational layer offers virtualized computing resources over the Internet. Users can rent servers, storage, and networking components, allowing for significant flexibility and control over the IT environment. Examples include Amazon EC2 and Google Compute Engine.
- Platform as a Service (PaaS): Positioned above IaaS, PaaS provides a platform for developers to build, deploy, and manage applications without worrying about the underlying infrastructure. This model includes development tools, databases, and middleware, streamlining the application lifecycle. Notable examples include Microsoft Azure and Heroku.
- Software as a Service (SaaS): This top layer delivers software applications over the Internet on a subscription basis. Users can access these applications via web browsers, minimizing the need for local

installations. Popular SaaS offerings include Google Workspace, Salesforce, and Microsoft 365.

2. Deployment Models

- The cloud reference model also outlines different deployment models, which define how cloud resources are provisioned and managed:
- Public Cloud: Services are delivered over the public Internet and shared across multiple organizations. Providers like AWS and Azure operate public clouds.
- Private Cloud: This model involves dedicated resources for a single organization, providing greater control and security. Private clouds can be managed on-premises or hosted by a third-party provider.
- Hybrid Cloud: Combining both public and private clouds, hybrid models allow organizations to leverage the benefits of both environments, facilitating data and application portability.

The cloud reference model serves as a vital tool for understanding the complexities of cloud computing. By categorizing services and deployment strategies, it aids organizations in selecting the right solutions for their needs, ultimately driving efficiency and innovation in a cloud-centric world.

2.5 Types of clouds

Cloud computing offers various deployment models that cater to different organizational needs. Understanding these types of clouds is essential for making informed decisions about resource management, security, and scalability. The three primary types of clouds are public, private, and hybrid, with a fourth emerging model, the multi-cloud. Each type has unique characteristics and use cases.

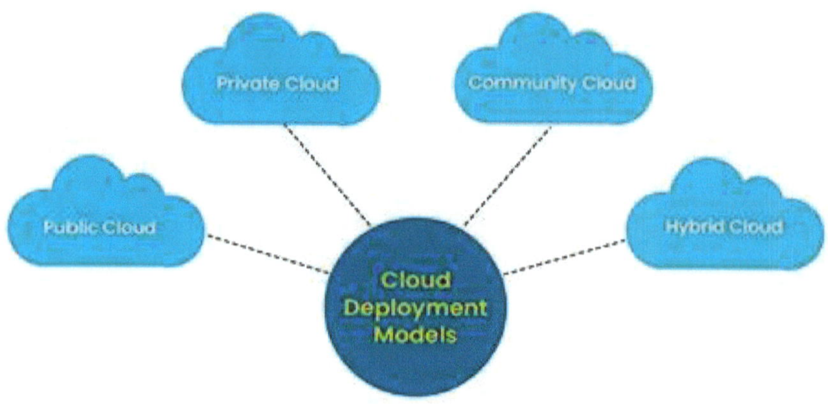

Figure: 2.1 Types of clouds

1. Public Cloud

Public clouds are owned and operated by third-party service providers who deliver computing resources over the Internet. These resources are shared among multiple organizations (often referred to as "tenants"), which allows for cost efficiencies and scalability.

Characteristics:

- Cost-Effective: Users pay only for what they use, eliminating the need for significant capital investment.
- Scalability: Public clouds can quickly scale resources up or down based on demand, making them ideal for fluctuating workloads.
- Accessibility: Services are available via the Internet, enabling users to access applications and data from anywhere.

Use Cases:

- Ideal for startups and small to medium-sized enterprises (SMEs) that need flexible resources without the overhead of managing infrastructure.
- Commonly used for web hosting, application development, and data backup.

2. Private Cloud

Private clouds are dedicated to a single organization, offering greater control and customization over the infrastructure. These clouds can be hosted on-premises or managed by a third-party provider.

Characteristics:

- Enhanced Security: Since the infrastructure is not shared with others, private clouds offer higher levels of security and compliance, making them suitable for industries with strict regulations.
- Customization: Organizations can tailor their private cloud environments to meet specific performance and operational requirements.

Use Cases:

- Frequently used by large enterprises, financial institutions, and healthcare organizations that handle sensitive data.
- Ideal for applications that require consistent performance, reliability, and governance.

3. Hybrid Cloud

Hybrid clouds combine public and private cloud resources, allowing organizations to take advantage of both models. This approach enables seamless data and application transfer between the two environments.

Characteristics:

- Flexibility: Organizations can choose where to run their workloads based on cost, performance, and compliance requirements.
- Optimized Resource Utilization: Businesses can keep sensitive data in a private cloud while leveraging the scalability of a public cloud for less sensitive workloads.

Use Cases:

- Suitable for companies that experience variable workloads, such as retail businesses that require extra resources during peak shopping seasons.
- Commonly used for disaster recovery solutions, where critical data can be stored in a private cloud while utilizing public cloud resources for

backup.

4. Multi-Cloud

The multi-cloud model involves using multiple cloud services from different providers. Organizations employ a combination of public and private clouds, often integrating services from various vendors.

Characteristics:

- Avoid Vendor Lock-In: Organizations can select the best services from multiple providers based on performance, cost, and features.
- Increased Resilience: By diversifying cloud services, businesses can enhance their redundancy and minimize the impact of service outages.

Use Cases:

- Common in enterprises that require specific functionalities from different cloud providers or want to optimize costs across various platforms.
- Useful for organizations that operate in multiple regions and need localized services.

Understanding the different types of clouds—public, private, hybrid, and multi-cloud—enables organizations to select the best deployment model for their unique requirements. By leveraging the strengths of each type, businesses can achieve greater flexibility, security, and efficiency in their cloud computing strategies. As cloud technology continues to evolve, organizations must adapt to these models to stay competitive in an increasingly digital landscape.

2.6 Economics of the cloud

The economics of cloud computing fundamentally transforms how organizations manage their IT resources and budget. By shifting from traditional capital expenditures (CapEx) to operational expenditures (OpEx), businesses can adopt a pay-as-you-go model, significantly reducing upfront costs associated with purchasing and maintaining hardware.

- Cost Savings: Organizations save on expenses related to physical infrastructure, power, cooling, and maintenance, allowing funds to be redirected toward innovation and growth.

- Scalability: The cloud offers unmatched scalability, enabling businesses to quickly adjust resources based on demand. This flexibility prevents over-provisioning and under-utilization, optimizing resource allocation and minimizing waste.
- Efficiency: With cloud services, companies can leverage advanced technologies—such as AI and machine learning—without significant investment, gaining a competitive edge.
- Risk Mitigation: Cloud providers often include built-in security and compliance features, reducing the risks associated with data breaches and regulatory penalties, which can be costly for businesses.

The economics of the cloud empowers organizations to operate more efficiently, reduce costs, and focus on strategic initiatives, making cloud computing a vital component of modern business strategy.

2.7 Open challengesCloud computing at a glance

Cloud computing has revolutionized the way businesses and individuals access and manage resources, but it also presents a variety of open challenges that need to be addressed for optimal performance and security. Here are some key challenges:

- Security and Privacy: Ensuring data security and user privacy remains a top concern. Data breaches, unauthorized access, and compliance with regulations like GDPR and HIPAA pose significant risks.
- Data Management: Efficiently managing large volumes of data, including storage, retrieval, and analytics, is critical. Organizations must address issues related to data consistency, integrity, and lifecycle management.
- Vendor Lock-In: Many organizations face challenges related to dependency on specific cloud providers. This can limit flexibility and complicate migration to other platforms or services.
- Cost Management: While cloud services can be cost-effective, unpredictable costs can arise from scaling and usage. Organizations need effective strategies for budgeting and monitoring cloud expenses.
- Service Reliability and Downtime: Ensuring high availability and minimizing downtime are crucial. Organizations must consider the impact of service outages and develop strategies for redundancy and failover.
- Performance Optimization: Achieving optimal performance in cloud environments can be challenging due to varying workloads, latency

issues, and network bandwidth constraints.

- Interoperability: Integrating different cloud services and platforms can be complex. Organizations need to ensure that various systems can work together seamlessly.
- Compliance and Legal Issues: Navigating the legal landscape of cloud computing, including data residency requirements and compliance standards, presents ongoing challenges for organizations.
- Skill Shortages: There is a growing demand for skilled professionals who can manage cloud infrastructures. Organizations may struggle to find and retain talent with the necessary expertise.
- Environmental Impact: As cloud computing continues to grow, the environmental footprint of data centers and energy consumption becomes a concern. Sustainable practices are needed to minimize this impact.

Addressing these challenges requires a multi-faceted approach involving technological innovation, strategic planning, and continuous improvement. As cloud computing evolves, organizations must stay informed and adaptable to leverage its full potential while mitigating risks.

2.8 Historical developments

Cloud computing has evolved significantly over the past few decades, shaping the way businesses and individuals interact with technology. Its journey can be traced through several key developments and milestones.

1. Early Concepts (1960s-1970s)

The roots of cloud computing date back to the 1960s with the concept of time-sharing systems, where multiple users could access a single mainframe computer. Visionaries like J.C.R. Licklider imagined a future where users could access data and applications remotely. The development of ARPANET in the late 1960s laid the groundwork for networked computing.

2. Emergence of Virtualization (1970s-1980s)

In the 1970s, IBM developed virtualization technologies that allowed a single physical server to host multiple virtual machines (VMs). This innovation enabled better resource utilization and laid the foundation for modern cloud infrastructures. By the 1980s, virtualization began to gain traction in enterprise settings, allowing organizations to run multiple operating systems on one machine.

3. The Internet Boom (1990s)

The widespread adoption of the internet in the 1990s was a turning point for cloud computing. The advent of web-based applications shifted how software was delivered. Companies like Salesforce, founded in 1999, pioneered Software as a Service (SaaS), offering applications over the internet instead of traditional installation methods. This shift marked the beginning of cloud-based services as we know them today.

4. The Rise of Infrastructure as a Service (2000s)

In the early 2000s, the cloud computing model began to take shape. Amazon Web Services (AWS) launched in 2006, introducing Infrastructure as a Service (IaaS) with its Elastic Compute Cloud (EC2). This service allowed businesses to rent computing power on-demand, revolutionizing how companies approached IT infrastructure. Other tech giants, including Google and Microsoft, followed suit, launching their cloud offerings.

5. Mainstream Adoption (2010s)

By the 2010s, cloud computing became mainstream, with businesses of all sizes adopting cloud solutions. The emergence of Public, Private, and Hybrid clouds provided organizations with flexible options to suit their needs. Companies increasingly recognized the benefits of scalability, cost-effectiveness, and improved collaboration.

Key players like Microsoft Azure and Google Cloud Platform expanded their services, offering a wide array of solutions, including machine learning, big data analytics, and Internet of Things (IoT) capabilities. Security concerns also prompted advancements in encryption and compliance measures, addressing the evolving landscape of data protection.

6. Multi-Cloud and Serverless Computing (Late 2010s-2020s)

The late 2010s saw the rise of multi-cloud strategies, where organizations leveraged services from multiple cloud providers to enhance resilience and avoid vendor lock-in. Serverless computing emerged as a new paradigm, allowing developers to build applications without managing infrastructure, further simplifying deployment and scaling.

7. Current Trends and Future Directions

As of the early 2020s, cloud computing continues to evolve, with a focus on artificial intelligence, machine learning, and edge computing. Organizations are increasingly prioritizing sustainability and energy efficiency in their cloud strategies. The COVID-19 pandemic accelerated digital transformation, pushing businesses to adopt cloud solutions rapidly.

The historical development of cloud computing reflects a journey of innovation driven by technological advancements and changing business needs. From early time-sharing systems to today's robust cloud ecosystems, the evolution of cloud computing has fundamentally transformed how we access and utilize technology, shaping the future of work and collaboration. As the landscape continues to change, ongoing advancements will likely redefine cloud computing's role in the digital age.

2.9 Building cloud computing environments

Creating effective cloud computing environments involves a strategic approach that encompasses various layers of architecture, technology selection, and operational management. The goal is to establish a robust, scalable, and secure infrastructure that meets the diverse needs of businesses. Below are key considerations and steps involved in building a cloud computing environment.

1. Define Objectives and Requirements

Before initiating the build process, it's essential to clearly define the objectives of the cloud environment. Determine what workloads will run in the cloud—be it applications, storage, or development environments. Understanding the specific requirements, such as performance, scalability, and compliance, will guide the design and technology choices.

2. Choose a Cloud Model

Cloud environments can be categorized into three primary models:

- Public Cloud: Services are provided over the internet and shared among multiple organizations. This model is cost-effective and scalable but may raise concerns about data security and compliance.
- Private Cloud: This model involves dedicated resources for a single organization, offering greater control and security. However, it requires significant investment and maintenance.
- Hybrid Cloud: Combining public and private clouds, this model provides flexibility, allowing organizations to scale resources and manage workloads according to varying demands.
- Selecting the appropriate model depends on the organization's specific needs, budget, and regulatory requirements.

3. Select Cloud Service Providers

Choosing the right cloud service provider (CSP) is critical. Major providers like Amazon Web Services (AWS), Microsoft Azure, and Google Cloud Platform (GCP) offer a range of services, including Infrastructure as a Service (IaaS), Platform as a Service (PaaS), and Software as a Service

(SaaS). Evaluate providers based on:

- Service Offerings: Ensure they offer the necessary tools and services to support your objectives.
- Security Measures: Review their security protocols, compliance certifications, and data protection policies.
- Pricing Structure: Understand the cost implications of their pricing models and evaluate potential hidden costs.

4. Design the Architecture

A well-architected cloud environment should include the following components:

- Compute Resources: Choose virtual machines or containers based on workload requirements. Consider auto-scaling capabilities for dynamic resource allocation.
- Storage Solutions: Select appropriate storage options—block storage, object storage, or file storage—depending on data access patterns and performance needs.
- Networking: Design a secure and efficient network architecture, including Virtual Private Clouds (VPCs), subnets, and firewalls to manage traffic and enhance security.
- Backup and Disaster Recovery: Implement solutions for data redundancy, backup, and disaster recovery to ensure business continuity.

5. Implement Security Measures

- Security is paramount in cloud environments. Incorporate a multi-layered security approach, including:
- Identity and Access Management (IAM): Use IAM policies to control user access and permissions.
- Encryption: Encrypt data at rest and in transit to protect sensitive information.
- Monitoring and Auditing: Utilize tools for continuous monitoring, logging, and auditing to detect and respond to security incidents promptly.

6. Testing and Optimization

Before going live, conduct thorough testing to ensure that the cloud environment meets performance, security, and scalability requirements. Performance testing, load testing, and security assessments will help identify potential bottlenecks and vulnerabilities.

7. Training and Management

Train your team on managing and optimizing the cloud environment. Continuous education is essential to keep up with evolving technologies and best practices.

Building a cloud computing environment is a complex but rewarding endeavor. By carefully defining objectives, selecting the right cloud model and provider, designing a secure architecture, and implementing robust management practices, organizations can leverage the full potential of cloud computing. This approach not only enhances operational efficiency but also positions businesses to adapt quickly to changing market demands.

2.10 The cloud reference model

The cloud reference model provides a framework to understand cloud computing's architecture, services, and deployment strategies. It delineates various layers and components that facilitate effective cloud service delivery, ensuring consistency and interoperability across different cloud environments.

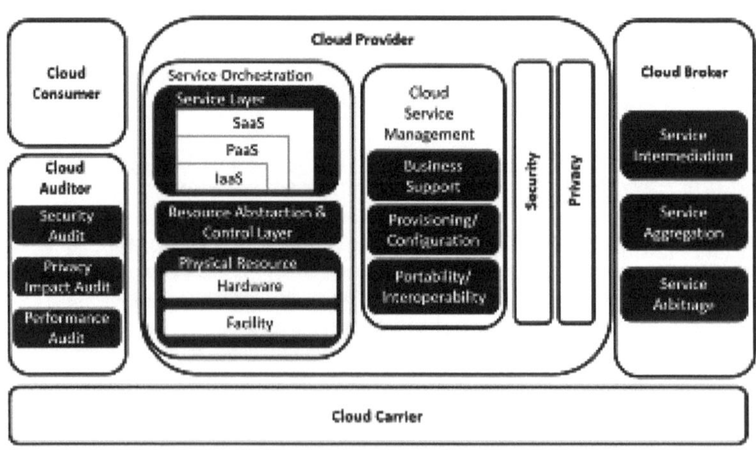

Figure 2.2 The cloud reference model

Layers of the Cloud Reference Model

- Physical Layer: At the foundation of the model is the physical layer, which encompasses the hardware and infrastructure that support cloud services. This includes data centers, servers, storage devices, and networking equipment. These resources are crucial as they provide the underlying capability for processing, storage, and data transfer. Virtualization technologies often sit on top of this layer, allowing multiple virtual machines to run on a single physical server.
- Infrastructure as a Service (IaaS): Above the physical layer is IaaS, where cloud providers offer virtualized computing resources over the internet. Users can rent virtual machines, storage, and networks, allowing them to scale their infrastructure without the need for physical hardware. Key benefits include flexibility, scalability, and cost-effectiveness. Prominent IaaS providers include Amazon Web Services (AWS) EC2, Google Cloud Compute Engine, and Microsoft Azure.
- Platform as a Service (PaaS): PaaS provides a platform allowing developers to build, test, and deploy applications without managing the underlying infrastructure. This layer includes development frameworks, databases, middleware, and tools for application management. PaaS streamlines the development process, enabling faster time-to-market for applications. Examples include Google App Engine and Heroku.
- Software as a Service (SaaS): SaaS delivers software applications over the internet, allowing users to access them via web browsers without installing or maintaining them on local devices. This layer abstracts the complexities of infrastructure and application management. Common examples include Google Workspace, Microsoft 365, and Salesforce. SaaS solutions are subscription-based, offering easy scalability and accessibility.
- Function as a Service (FaaS): Also known as serverless computing, FaaS allows developers to run code in response to events without provisioning or managing servers. This model abstracts away the infrastructure concerns, enabling rapid development and deployment of applications. It's particularly useful for event-driven architectures and microservices. Examples include AWS Lambda and Azure Functions.

Deployment Models

The cloud reference model also encompasses deployment models, defining how cloud services are made available:

- Public Cloud: Services are offered over the internet and shared across multiple organizations. This model is cost-effective and scalable but may raise concerns over data security and compliance.
- Private Cloud: Dedicated resources for a single organization, either on-premises or hosted by a third party. This model offers greater control over security and compliance.
- Hybrid Cloud: Combines both public and private clouds, allowing data and applications to be shared between them. This model provides flexibility and scalability while maintaining control over sensitive data.
- Multi-Cloud: Involves using services from multiple cloud providers, enhancing redundancy and reducing vendor lock-in.

The cloud reference model serves as a blueprint for understanding the various layers and services in cloud computing. By clarifying the distinctions between IaaS, PaaS, SaaS, and FaaS, as well as different deployment models, it helps organizations make informed decisions about their cloud strategies, optimize their operations, and leverage cloud technologies effectively.

2.11 Types of clouds

Cloud computing has transformed how organizations store, manage, and process data by providing flexible and scalable solutions. Various types of cloud environments cater to different needs, each offering unique advantages. The primary classifications are public, private, hybrid, and multi-cloud. Here's a closer look at each type:

1. Public Cloud

Public clouds are services offered over the internet and shared across multiple organizations. They are managed by third-party providers, such as Amazon Web Services (AWS), Microsoft Azure, and Google Cloud Platform (GCP). Key features include:

- Cost-Effectiveness: Users pay for the resources they consume, eliminating the need for significant upfront investment in hardware.
- Scalability: Resources can be quickly scaled up or down to meet demand, making it ideal for fluctuating workloads.
- Maintenance-Free: The cloud provider handles maintenance, updates, and security, allowing users to focus on their core business functions.

However, concerns over data security and compliance can arise since data is stored offsite and shared with other customers.

2. Private Cloud

A private cloud is dedicated solely to a single organization. It can be hosted on-premises or by a third-party provider. This model offers several benefits:

- Enhanced Security: Since resources are not shared with other organizations, private clouds provide greater control over data security and compliance with regulatory requirements.
- Customization: Organizations can tailor the cloud environment to their specific needs, configuring hardware and software to suit their applications.
- Predictable Performance: With dedicated resources, organizations can achieve consistent performance levels, which is crucial for mission-critical applications.

However, private clouds often come with higher costs, as organizations must invest in the necessary infrastructure and management.

3. Hybrid Cloud

The hybrid cloud model combines elements of both public and private clouds, allowing data and applications to be shared between them. This approach offers:

- Flexibility: Organizations can run sensitive workloads in the private cloud while leveraging the public cloud for less critical operations, optimizing resource use.
- Cost Efficiency: Businesses can reduce costs by utilizing public cloud resources for variable workloads while keeping essential data secure in a private cloud.
- Improved Disaster Recovery: Hybrid clouds can enhance disaster recovery strategies by providing multiple storage and backup options across different environments.

However, managing a hybrid cloud can be complex, requiring robust integration and orchestration strategies.

4. Multi-Cloud

Multi-cloud refers to the use of services from multiple cloud providers, without necessarily combining public and private clouds. This model is characterized by:

- Avoiding Vendor Lock-In: Organizations can choose the best services from various providers, reducing dependency on a single vendor.
- Enhanced Redundancy and Reliability: Utilizing multiple clouds can improve service availability and performance by distributing workloads across various platforms.
- Optimized Costs: Companies can leverage competitive pricing across different providers, allowing them to select cost-effective solutions for specific needs.

However, managing multiple cloud environments can complicate governance, security, and compliance, requiring advanced management tools and strategies.

The choice between public, private, hybrid, and multi-cloud models depends on an organization's specific requirements, including security needs, budget constraints, and workload variability. Understanding these types allows businesses to make informed decisions about their cloud strategy, enabling them to leverage the benefits of cloud computing effectively while addressing their unique challenges. As cloud technology continues to evolve, these models will adapt to meet emerging demands, making cloud computing an essential aspect of modern IT infrastructure.

2.12 Economics of the cloud

The economics of cloud computing fundamentally reshapes how organizations manage IT costs and resources. By transitioning to the cloud, businesses shift from capital expenditure (CapEx) to operational expenditure (OpEx), enabling them to pay for resources on a subscription basis rather than investing heavily in hardware and infrastructure upfront. This model enhances financial flexibility, allowing companies to scale resources up or down based on demand.

Additionally, cloud providers benefit from economies of scale, passing cost savings to customers through lower prices. The competitive landscape fosters innovation and pricing competition, further driving down costs.

Cost predictability is another advantage; organizations can better forecast expenses with pay-as-you-go models, avoiding unexpected spikes in IT spending. Moreover, cloud solutions often include maintenance, security, and updates, reducing the burden on internal IT teams.

However, businesses must consider potential hidden costs, such as data transfer fees and costs associated with managing multiple cloud services. Effective cloud governance and cost management strategies are essential to maximize the economic benefits while minimizing risks. Overall, the cloud offers a more agile, cost-effective approach to IT that aligns with modern business needs.

2.13 Open challenges

Despite the significant benefits of cloud computing, several open challenges remain that organizations must navigate.

1. Security and Privacy:

As businesses migrate sensitive data to the cloud, ensuring data security and compliance with regulations (like GDPR) becomes paramount. Cloud providers implement various security measures, but vulnerabilities still exist, making data breaches a significant concern.

2. Vendor Lock-In:

Organizations often face difficulties when trying to switch providers due to proprietary technologies and data formats. This reliance can limit flexibility and increase costs in the long run.

3. Interoperability:

With many organizations using multiple cloud services, ensuring seamless integration and communication between different platforms remains a challenge. Lack of standardized protocols can hinder collaboration and data sharing.

4. Performance and Reliability:

Cloud services can experience downtime, affecting business operations. Organizations must ensure that their cloud providers meet service-level agreements (SLAs) for uptime and performance.

5. Cost Management:

While cloud solutions can reduce costs, managing and predicting expenses can be complex, especially in multi-cloud environments. Without proper oversight, organizations may face unexpected charges.

Addressing these challenges is crucial for maximizing the potential of cloud computing while safeguarding organizational interests.

CHAPTER THREE

Principles of Parallel and Distributed Computing

3.1 Principles of Parallel and Distributed Computing

Parallel and distributed computing are key paradigms in modern computing, enabling systems to process large amounts of data efficiently and solve complex problems. While both involve multiple computing resources, they do so in different ways and are governed by several fundamental principles.

1. Decomposition

Decomposition is the process of breaking down a large problem into smaller, manageable sub-problems that can be solved simultaneously. In parallel computing, tasks are divided among multiple processors within a single system. In distributed computing, tasks are distributed across different machines, often located in different geographical locations. Effective decomposition ensures that tasks can be executed independently, maximizing resource utilization.

2. Communication

Communication is crucial in both parallel and distributed systems. In parallel computing, processes typically communicate through shared memory or inter-process communication (IPC) mechanisms, allowing for fast data exchange. In distributed computing, communication often occurs over a network, requiring efficient protocols to handle latency and bandwidth constraints. Understanding the trade-offs between communication costs and computation is essential for optimizing performance.

3. Synchronization

Synchronization ensures that processes coordinate their activities to avoid conflicts, particularly when they access shared resources. In parallel computing, synchronization mechanisms (such as locks, semaphores, and barriers) help manage concurrent access to shared memory. In distributed systems, synchronization can be more complex due to the lack of a global clock, requiring algorithms like consensus protocols to ensure consistency across nodes.

4. Scalability

Scalability refers to a system's ability to handle an increasing amount of work by adding more resources. In parallel computing, scalability is often limited by the shared memory architecture and communication overhead among processors. Distributed systems, however, can achieve greater scalability by adding more nodes to the network, allowing for a more extensive distribution of workloads. Understanding how to design algorithms that scale efficiently is vital for both paradigms.

5. Fault Tolerance

Fault tolerance is the ability of a system to continue operating properly in the event of a failure. In parallel computing, if a processor fails, it may impact the entire computation. Distributed systems, however, are designed with redundancy, allowing them to recover from node failures without losing overall system functionality. Implementing strategies such as replication and checkpointing can enhance fault tolerance in distributed environments.

6. Load Balancing

Load balancing ensures that all computing resources are utilized efficiently, preventing some nodes from being overworked while others are idle. In parallel computing, load balancing algorithms distribute tasks among processors to optimize performance. In distributed computing, it involves distributing workloads across multiple nodes to prevent bottlenecks. Effective load balancing contributes to higher system efficiency and reduced execution time.

7. Transparency

Transparency refers to the abstraction that hides the complexities of the underlying system from users. In parallel computing, this might involve providing a uniform interface for accessing shared memory, while in distributed computing, it might mean presenting a single system view despite multiple underlying nodes. Achieving transparency simplifies application development and improves usability.

The principles of parallel and distributed computing are foundational to developing efficient, robust systems that can tackle complex problems.

By leveraging decomposition, effective communication, synchronization, scalability, fault tolerance, load balancing, and transparency, developers can create systems that maximize resource utilization and enhance performance. Understanding these principles is essential for navigating the evolving landscape of computing technologies.

3.2 Parallel vs. distributed computing

Parallel and distributed computing are two essential paradigms in computer science that enable the efficient processing of large datasets and complex computations. While they share some similarities, they differ significantly in their architecture, execution model, and application scenarios. Here's a breakdown of their key differences and characteristics.

Definition

Parallel Computing refers to the simultaneous execution of multiple calculations or processes within a single computer system. It typically involves multiple processors or cores working together on a shared task, utilizing shared memory to coordinate their activities.

Distributed Computing, on the other hand, involves multiple independent computers (or nodes) that communicate and collaborate to solve a problem. These nodes may be physically separated and connected via a network, and they operate independently, often with their own local memory.

Architecture

In parallel computing, all processors share the same memory space, which allows for fast communication between them. This architecture can be homogeneous (identical processors) or heterogeneous (different types of processors). The shared memory model facilitates easy access to data, but it can lead to challenges such as contention and bottlenecks.

In contrast, distributed computing consists of multiple independent systems that do not share memory. Each node has its own memory and may run its own operating system. Communication between nodes typically occurs over a network using message-passing protocols, which can introduce latency and increase complexity in managing data consistency.

Execution Model

Parallel computing executes tasks simultaneously, often using a single algorithm that divides the workload across multiple processors. This model is well-suited for problems that can be easily divided into smaller, independent sub-tasks, such as numerical simulations or image processing.

Distributed computing, however, relies on coordination between nodes to achieve a common goal. Tasks are divided among different machines, and nodes may execute different algorithms. This model is ideal for applications that require high availability, fault tolerance, or scalability, such as cloud computing and big data processing.

Communication

Communication in parallel computing is typically faster because of the shared memory architecture. Processes can access shared data directly, which leads to lower latency. However, this also necessitates synchronization mechanisms to manage concurrent access, which can introduce complexity.

In distributed computing, communication occurs over a network, which can lead to higher latency and potential data transmission issues. Nodes must rely on message-passing protocols to share information, making the design of communication strategies crucial for system performance.

Scalability

Parallel computing has limitations in scalability. As more processors are added, the performance gains may diminish due to increased overhead from communication and synchronization. This phenomenon is often referred to as Amdahl's Law, which states that the potential speedup of a program is limited by the sequential portion of the task.

Distributed computing, however, offers greater scalability since new nodes can be added to the system without significant architectural changes. This scalability allows organizations to manage growing workloads effectively, making distributed systems ideal for large-scale applications.

Fault Tolerance

Fault tolerance is another critical difference. In parallel computing, a failure in one processor can halt the entire computation. Conversely, distributed systems are designed to be more resilient, allowing the remaining nodes to continue functioning even if one or more nodes fail. Techniques such as replication and redundancy enhance the fault tolerance of distributed systems.

In summary, parallel and distributed computing serve distinct purposes and cater to different types of problems. Parallel computing excels in scenarios requiring rapid, simultaneous processing within a single system, while distributed computing shines in applications that demand scalability, fault tolerance, and the ability to leverage multiple independent systems. Understanding these differences is essential for selecting the appropriate approach based on the specific requirements of a given task or application.

3.3 Elements of parallel computing

Parallel computing involves several key elements that facilitate efficient processing and problem-solving across multiple computational resources. Here are the primary elements:

1. Decomposition:

This involves breaking down a large problem into smaller, independent tasks that can be executed simultaneously. Effective decomposition is crucial for maximizing parallelism.

2. Concurrency:

Concurrency refers to the ability of a system to handle multiple tasks at once. In parallel computing, processes run concurrently, allowing for more efficient resource utilization.

3. Communication:

Processes often need to share data or coordinate actions. Communication mechanisms, such as shared memory or message-passing protocols, are essential for synchronization and data exchange among parallel tasks.

4. Synchronization:

This ensures that processes coordinate their operations, especially when accessing shared resources. Techniques like locks, semaphores, and barriers help manage concurrent access and prevent conflicts.

5. Load Balancing:

Distributing workloads evenly across processing units optimizes performance and minimizes idle time. Effective load balancing enhances resource utilization and reduces execution time.

6. Scalability:

The ability to maintain performance as more processing units are added is vital. Scalable systems efficiently handle increased workloads without significant degradation in speed.

These elements collectively enable parallel computing to solve complex problems more efficiently than traditional serial processing.

3.4 Elements of distributed computing

Distributed computing involves several key elements that enable multiple independent systems to collaborate effectively. Here are the primary components:

1. Nodes:

These are the individual computers or servers that make up the distributed system. Each node operates independently, with its own resources and local memory.

2. Communication:

Nodes communicate over a network using message-passing protocols. Efficient communication mechanisms are essential for sharing data and coordinating tasks, often employing APIs or middleware for seamless interaction.

3. Data Distribution:

Data is often distributed across multiple nodes, requiring strategies for partitioning and replication. Effective data distribution enhances performance and reliability, ensuring that nodes can access the information they need.

4. Fault Tolerance:

Distributed systems must be resilient to failures. Techniques such as redundancy, replication, and consensus algorithms help ensure that the system continues to function even if some nodes fail.

5. Scalability:

The system should efficiently accommodate growth by adding more nodes without significant performance loss. Scalable architectures allow for handling increasing workloads effectively.

6. Transparency:

Transparency in distributed computing hides the complexities of the underlying system from users, presenting a unified view despite the distribution of resources.

These elements work together to enable robust and efficient distributed computing environments.

3.5 Technologies for distributed computing

Distributed computing leverages various technologies to facilitate communication, data management, and resource sharing among multiple systems. Here are some key technologies:

1. Middleware:

Middleware acts as a bridge between different applications and services, providing essential services like messaging, authentication, and transaction management. Examples include Apache Kafka and RabbitMQ.

2. Remote Procedure Call (RPC):

RPC enables communication between distributed systems by allowing a program to execute procedures on another address space. Frameworks like gRPC simplify the process of building distributed applications.

3. Message Queues:

Message queuing systems, such as Amazon SQS and Apache ActiveMQ, allow asynchronous communication between distributed components, ensuring reliable message delivery even in the event of system failures.

4. Distributed Databases:

Technologies like Apache Cassandra and MongoDB support data distribution across multiple nodes, ensuring data consistency and availability while handling large volumes of data.

5. Containerization and Orchestration:

Tools like Docker and Kubernetes enable developers to deploy applications in isolated environments, manage resource allocation, and automate scaling across distributed systems.

6. Cloud Computing Platforms:

Services such as AWS, Google Cloud, and Microsoft Azure provide infrastructure and services that facilitate distributed computing, offering scalability and flexibility for various applications.

These technologies collectively enhance the efficiency and reliability of distributed computing systems.

CHAPTER FOUR

Virtualization

4.1 Virtualization Introduction

Distributed computing leverages various technologies to facilitate communication, data management, and resource sharing among multiple systems. Here are some key technologies:

1. Middleware:

Middleware acts as a bridge between different applications and services, providing essential services like messaging, authentication, and transaction management. Examples include Apache Kafka and RabbitMQ.

2. Remote Procedure Call (RPC):

RPC enables communication between distributed systems by allowing a program to execute procedures on another address space. Frameworks like gRPC simplify the process of building distributed applications.

3. Message Queues:

Message queuing systems, such as Amazon SQS and Apache ActiveMQ, allow asynchronous communication between distributed components, ensuring reliable message delivery even in the event of system failures.

4. Distributed Databases:

Technologies like Apache Cassandra and MongoDB support data distribution across multiple nodes, ensuring data consistency and availability while handling large volumes of data.

5. Containerization and Orchestration:

Tools like Docker and Kubernetes enable developers to deploy applications in isolated environments, manage resource allocation, and automate scaling across distributed systems.

6. Cloud Computing Platforms:

Services such as AWS, Google Cloud, and Microsoft Azure provide infrastructure and services that facilitate distributed computing, offering scalability and flexibility for various applications.

These technologies collectively enhance the efficiency and reliability of distributed computing systems.

4.2 Characteristics of virtualized environments

Virtualized environments have become integral to modern IT infrastructure, providing numerous benefits that enhance efficiency, flexibility, and scalability. Understanding the key characteristics of these environments is essential for leveraging their full potential. Here are the primary characteristics of virtualized environments:

1. Resource Abstraction

At the core of virtualization is the abstraction of physical hardware. Virtualized environments enable multiple virtual machines (VMs) to run on a single physical host, with each VM acting as an independent entity. This abstraction allows for the dynamic allocation of resources such as CPU, memory, and storage, facilitating better utilization of available hardware.

2. Isolation

Isolation is a fundamental characteristic of virtualized environments. Each VM operates independently, meaning that issues within one VM (such as crashes or security breaches) do not impact others. This isolation enhances security and stability, making it ideal for multi-tenant environments, such as cloud computing, where different customers' workloads can coexist safely on the same physical infrastructure.

3. Scalability

Virtualized environments are inherently scalable. Organizations can quickly add or remove VMs based on demand, allowing for efficient resource management. This elasticity is particularly beneficial in environments with fluctuating workloads, enabling businesses to respond to changing requirements without significant hardware investment.

4. Efficiency and Cost Savings

By maximizing resource utilization, virtualization reduces the need for physical hardware. Multiple VMs can run on a single server, leading to lower capital expenditures on hardware, reduced energy consumption, and decreased data center space requirements. Organizations can achieve significant cost savings while maintaining high performance.

5. Flexibility and Agility

Virtualization provides flexibility in deploying applications and services. New VMs can be created and configured in minutes, allowing organizations to rapidly provision resources for development, testing, and production. This agility accelerates time-to-market for applications and supports innovative business strategies.

6. Simplified Management

Virtualized environments often come with centralized management tools that simplify the administration of multiple VMs. These tools enable administrators to monitor performance, allocate resources, and manage backups from a single interface. Automation features can also reduce manual tasks, further streamlining operations.

7. Disaster Recovery and High Availability

Virtualization enhances disaster recovery (DR) capabilities. VMs can be easily replicated and backed up, allowing organizations to quickly recover from hardware failures or data loss. Many virtualization platforms offer built-in features for high availability, ensuring that VMs remain operational even in the event of a host failure.

8. Snapshot and Cloning Capabilities

Virtualized environments support snapshot and cloning functionalities, allowing administrators to capture the state of a VM at a specific point in time. Snapshots facilitate testing and development by enabling quick rollbacks to previous states. Cloning allows for rapid deployment of identical VMs, enhancing operational efficiency.

9. Network Virtualization

In addition to hardware resources, virtualization extends to networking. Network virtualization enables the creation of virtual networks that can operate independently of physical network configurations. This flexibility allows for dynamic network management, improving security and performance.

10. Integration with Cloud Technologies

Virtualization is foundational to cloud computing. Most cloud providers rely on virtualized environments to deliver Infrastructure as a Service (IaaS) and Platform as a Service (PaaS). This integration facilitates scalable, on-demand resources that can be accessed over the internet, making it easier for organizations to adopt cloud strategies.

The characteristics of virtualized environments—resource abstraction, isolation, scalability, efficiency, flexibility, simplified management, disaster recovery capabilities, snapshot functionalities, network virtualization, and integration with cloud technologies—collectively contribute to their widespread adoption in modern IT infrastructures. Understanding these traits helps organizations leverage virtualization effectively to enhance their operational efficiency, reduce costs, and support business growth. As technology continues to evolve, virtualized environments will play a crucial role in shaping the future of computing.

4.3 Taxonomy of virtualization techniques

Virtualization techniques have evolved significantly, enabling efficient resource utilization and management across diverse computing environments. The taxonomy of virtualization can be categorized based on several criteria, including the type of resources being virtualized, the architectural approach, and the level of abstraction. Here's a detailed overview of the primary categories and their subtypes.

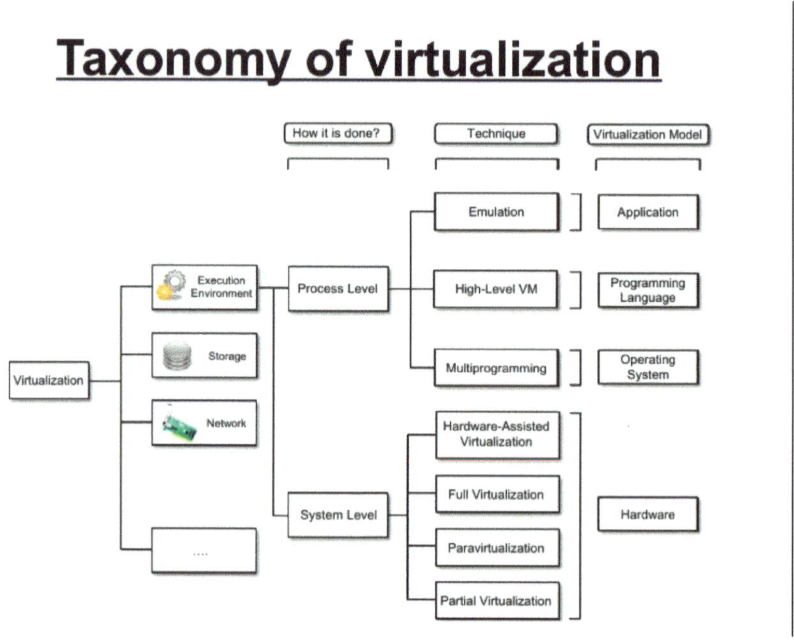

Figure: 4.1 Taxonomy of Virtualization Techniques in Cloud Computing

1. Type of Virtualization

a. Server Virtualization

Server virtualization is the most common form, where physical servers are divided into multiple virtual machines (VMs). Each VM operates independently with its own operating system and applications. Techniques include:

- Full Virtualization: Emulates complete hardware, allowing unmodified guest OS installations. Examples include VMware ESXi and Microsoft Hyper-V.
- Paravirtualization: Requires guest OS modifications to interact with the hypervisor directly, improving performance. Examples include Xen and KVM.
- OS-Level Virtualization: Virtualizes the operating system kernel, enabling multiple isolated user-space instances. Examples include Docker and LXC (Linux Containers).

b. Desktop Virtualization

Desktop virtualization allows users to run desktop environments on centralized servers, accessible from various devices. Techniques include:

- Virtual Desktop Infrastructure (VDI): Hosts desktop operating systems on a server, delivering them to end-users via remote access. Examples include VMware Horizon and Citrix Virtual Apps.
- Remote Desktop Services (RDS): Allows multiple users to share a single desktop environment, typically used for application delivery.

c. Application Virtualization

Application virtualization separates applications from the underlying operating system, allowing them to run in isolated environments. Techniques include:

- Streaming: Applications are delivered on-demand to the user's device, running as if installed locally. Examples include Microsoft App-V and Citrix XenApp.
- Containerization: Packages applications and their dependencies into containers, enabling consistent deployment across environments. Examples include Docker and Kubernetes.

2. Architectural Approach

a. Type 1 Hypervisors (Bare-Metal)

These hypervisors run directly on physical hardware without an underlying OS. They provide better performance and resource management. Examples include VMware ESXi, Microsoft Hyper-V, and Xen.

b. Type 2 Hypervisors (Hosted)

These hypervisors operate on top of an existing operating system, making them easier to install and manage but potentially less efficient than Type 1 hypervisors. Examples include VMware Workstation and Oracle VirtualBox.

3. Level of Abstraction

a. Hardware Virtualization

This involves creating virtual representations of physical hardware components, allowing multiple VMs to share CPU, memory, and storage resources. This is the foundation of most virtualization technologies.

b. Network Virtualization

Network virtualization abstracts networking resources, creating virtual networks that operate independently of physical networks. Techniques include:

- Virtual LANs (VLANs): Segmenting a physical network into multiple logical networks.
- Software-Defined Networking (SDN): Separates the control plane from the data plane, enabling centralized management of network resources.

c. Storage Virtualization

Storage virtualization abstracts physical storage resources, pooling them into a single logical unit. This facilitates easier management and allocation of storage resources. Techniques include:

- Block Storage Virtualization: Abstracts storage devices into a single logical unit for use by multiple servers.
- File Storage Virtualization: Provides a unified interface for accessing files across different storage systems.

4. Cloud Virtualization

In cloud computing, virtualization is a foundational technology that enables on-demand resource provisioning and scalability. It allows cloud providers to deliver services efficiently through virtualized environments, supporting Infrastructure as a Service (IaaS) and Platform as a Service (PaaS) models.

The taxonomy of virtualization techniques encompasses various categories and subtypes, each tailored to specific needs and use cases. From server and desktop virtualization to application and storage virtualization, these techniques play a crucial role in modern IT infrastructure, enhancing resource efficiency, flexibility, and scalability. As technology continues to advance, the landscape of virtualization will evolve, introducing new methods and tools that further improve operational efficiencies and support diverse computing environments.

4.4 Virtualization and cloud computing

Virtualization and cloud computing are closely intertwined technologies that have revolutionized the way businesses manage IT resources. Understanding their relationship, distinct features, and applications is essential for organizations looking to optimize their infrastructure and achieve greater efficiency.

What is Virtualization?

Virtualization is a technology that enables the creation of virtual instances of computing resources, such as servers, storage devices, and networks. This is achieved through a software layer called a hypervisor, which abstracts physical hardware and allows multiple virtual machines (VMs) to run on a single physical host. Each VM operates independently, with its own operating system and applications, as if it were a separate physical machine.

Types of Virtualization:

- Server Virtualization: The most common form, where multiple VMs share a single physical server. This can be achieved through:
- Full Virtualization: Complete emulation of hardware, allowing unmodified operating systems to run.
- Paravirtualization: Requires guest OS modifications for better performance.
- OS-Level Virtualization: Runs multiple isolated user-space instances on a single OS kernel, such as containers (e.g., Docker).
- Desktop Virtualization: Delivers desktop environments from centralized servers to end-users. Key types include:
- Virtual Desktop Infrastructure (VDI): Hosts desktop operating systems on servers.
- Remote Desktop Services (RDS): Allows multiple users to access a shared desktop environment.
- Application Virtualization: Abstracts applications from the underlying OS, enabling isolated execution. Examples include application streaming

and containers.
- Network and Storage Virtualization: Abstracts networking and storage resources to create logical representations that simplify management and enhance resource utilization.

What is Cloud Computing?

Cloud Computing is the delivery of computing services—such as servers, storage, databases, networking, software, and analytics—over the internet (the cloud). It allows organizations to access and use technology resources on-demand without the need for extensive on-premises infrastructure.

Deployment Models:

- Public Cloud: Services are provided over the internet by third-party providers (e.g., AWS, Google Cloud, Microsoft Azure). Resources are shared among multiple customers, offering cost-effectiveness and scalability.
- Private Cloud: Services are dedicated to a single organization, either hosted on-premises or by a third-party provider. This model provides greater control, security, and compliance.
- Hybrid Cloud: Combines public and private clouds, allowing data and applications to be shared between them. This model offers flexibility and enables organizations to leverage the benefits of both environments.
- Multi-Cloud: Involves using multiple cloud services from different providers. This approach helps avoid vendor lock-in and allows organizations to choose the best services for their needs.

The Relationship Between Virtualization and Cloud Computing

- Virtualization is a foundational technology that enables cloud computing. It allows cloud providers to efficiently manage and allocate resources across multiple customers. Here's how virtualization supports cloud computing:
- Resource Efficiency: By virtualizing physical hardware, cloud providers can maximize resource utilization, running multiple VMs on a single server. This leads to reduced costs and energy consumption.
- Scalability: Virtualization enables rapid provisioning of resources. Organizations can quickly scale their infrastructure up or down based on demand, a critical feature for cloud services.

- Flexibility: Virtualized environments allow for the easy deployment of new applications and services. Organizations can quickly create and configure VMs to meet changing business needs.
- Isolation and Security: Each VM operates independently, providing a level of isolation that enhances security. This is particularly important in multi-tenant environments, where different customers share the same physical infrastructure.
- Disaster Recovery and High Availability: Virtualization facilitates backup and recovery processes. VMs can be easily replicated and moved to different locations, enhancing disaster recovery strategies and ensuring high availability.

Benefits of Virtualization and Cloud Computing

- Cost Savings: Both technologies reduce the need for physical hardware and associated maintenance costs. Organizations can shift from capital expenditures (CapEx) to operational expenditures (OpEx), paying only for the resources they use.
- Improved Agility: Virtualization and cloud computing enable organizations to deploy applications and services quickly, fostering innovation and responsiveness to market changes.
- Simplified Management: Centralized management tools streamline the administration of resources, making it easier for IT teams to monitor performance, allocate resources, and implement updates.
- Enhanced Collaboration. Cloud computing facilitates collaboration by allowing teams to access applications and data from anywhere with an internet connection, supporting remote work and global teams.

Challenges and Considerations

While virtualization and cloud computing offer numerous benefits, organizations must also consider potential challenges, such as:

- Security Risks: Storing data in the cloud can expose it to security threats. Organizations must implement robust security measures to protect sensitive information.
- Compliance Issues: Regulatory requirements may complicate data storage and management in cloud environments. Organizations need to ensure compliance with industry standards.

- Vendor Lock-In: Relying on a single cloud provider can create challenges in migrating data and applications. Multi-cloud strategies can mitigate this risk.
- Performance Concerns: Network latency and bandwidth limitations can impact the performance of cloud-based applications. Organizations should assess their network infrastructure before migrating to the cloud.

Virtualization and cloud computing are pivotal in modern IT infrastructure, driving efficiency, flexibility, and scalability. By understanding their relationship and leveraging their combined strengths, organizations can optimize their resource management, reduce costs, and enhance their operational agility. As technology continues to advance, the integration of virtualization and cloud computing will remain a key strategy for organizations looking to thrive in a rapidly changing digital landscape.

4.5 Pros and cons of virtualization

Virtualization is a powerful technology that allows multiple virtual instances of computing resources to run on a single physical machine. While it offers numerous advantages, it also comes with some drawbacks. Understanding both the pros and cons is essential for organizations considering virtualization as part of their IT strategy.

Pros of Virtualization

- Resource Optimization: Virtualization enables better utilization of physical hardware by allowing multiple virtual machines (VMs) to run on a single server. This reduces the need for additional hardware, lowering capital expenditure and operational costs.
- Scalability: Virtual environments can be quickly scaled up or down based on demand. New VMs can be provisioned within minutes, making it easier for businesses to adapt to changing workloads and business needs.
- Isolation and Security: Each VM operates independently, providing a level of isolation that enhances security. Issues in one VM, such as crashes or security breaches, do not affect others, making it a robust solution for multi-tenant environments.
- Simplified Management: Centralized management tools enable administrators to monitor and manage multiple VMs from a single interface. This streamlines tasks such as updates, backups, and resource allocation, improving overall IT efficiency.

- Disaster Recovery and High Availability: Virtualization simplifies backup and recovery processes. VMs can be easily replicated and moved to different physical hosts, enabling quick recovery from hardware failures and ensuring high availability of critical applications.
- Development and Testing Environments: Virtualization allows developers to create multiple isolated environments for testing applications without the need for additional hardware. This flexibility accelerates development cycles and reduces the risk of errors in production environments.
- Energy Efficiency: By consolidating workloads on fewer physical servers, virtualization can lead to significant reductions in energy consumption, contributing to greener IT practices.

Cons of Virtualization

- Initial Setup Costs: While virtualization reduces long-term costs, the initial investment in virtualization software, licensing, and hardware upgrades can be significant. Organizations need to carefully consider their budget before adopting virtualization.
- Complexity: Managing a virtualized environment can be more complex than traditional environments. IT teams must be knowledgeable about virtualization technologies, and the increased complexity can lead to potential misconfigurations and errors.
- Performance Overhead: Virtualization introduces some performance overhead due to the hypervisor layer. Although modern hypervisors are optimized for performance, some resource-intensive applications may experience latency or reduced performance compared to running directly on physical hardware.
- Resource Contention: Multiple VMs sharing the same physical resources can lead to contention, where one VM consumes excessive resources, affecting the performance of others. Proper resource allocation and monitoring are essential to mitigate this issue.
- Security Risks: While VMs are isolated, vulnerabilities in the hypervisor can expose the entire environment to security risks. Organizations must implement robust security measures and keep virtualization software up to date to protect against potential threats.
- Vendor Lock-In: Organizations may become dependent on specific virtualization vendors for their infrastructure. This can lead to

challenges if they wish to migrate to different solutions in the future, as moving VMs between different hypervisors can be complex.

- Licensing and Compliance: Virtualization can complicate software licensing and compliance. Organizations must ensure that they adhere to licensing agreements for both the virtualization software and the applications running on VMs.

Virtualization offers numerous benefits, including resource optimization, scalability, and improved disaster recovery capabilities. However, organizations must also consider the potential downsides, such as initial setup costs, complexity, and performance overhead. By weighing the pros and cons, businesses can make informed decisions about adopting virtualization technology and effectively leverage its advantages while mitigating associated risks. Ultimately, the successful implementation of virtualization requires careful planning, ongoing management, and a clear understanding of organizational needs.

4.6 Technology examples

Here are some notable technology examples across various domains:

1. Virtualization Technologies

- VMware: A leader in server virtualization, VMware offers solutions like VMware vSphere for creating and managing virtual machines.
- Microsoft Hyper-V: A hypervisor that enables the creation of virtualized server environments, allowing multiple OS instances on a single physical server.
- Docker: A platform for developing, shipping, and running applications in containers, facilitating application virtualization and deployment.

2. Cloud Computing Platforms

- Amazon Web Services (AWS): Provides a comprehensive suite of cloud services, including compute power, storage, and databases, enabling scalable applications.
- Google Cloud Platform (GCP): Offers services for computing, data storage, and machine learning, with a strong focus on analytics and big data.
- Microsoft Azure: A cloud platform that integrates various services, including IaaS and PaaS, for building, deploying, and managing

applications.

3. Networking Technologies

- Cisco: Known for networking hardware and software solutions, Cisco provides routers, switches, and security solutions for enterprises.
- Software-Defined Networking (SDN): Technologies like OpenFlow allow for the programmatic management of networks, enhancing flexibility and efficiency.

4. Data Storage Solutions

- NetApp: Offers storage solutions that include data management and cloud-integrated storage systems for enterprises.
- Dell EMC: Provides a wide range of storage products, including flash storage and hyper-converged infrastructure.

These examples illustrate the breadth of technologies that drive efficiency, scalability, and innovation in today's digital landscape.

CHAPTER FIVE

Virtual Machines Provisioning and Migration Services

5.1 Virtual Machines Provisioning

Provisioning virtual machines (VMs) is a fundamental process in virtualization and cloud computing, enabling organizations to create, configure, and deploy VMs quickly and efficiently. This process is crucial for maximizing resource utilization, ensuring scalability, and meeting the dynamic demands of applications and users. Below is an overview of the key aspects of VM provisioning, including its types, methods, tools, and best practices.

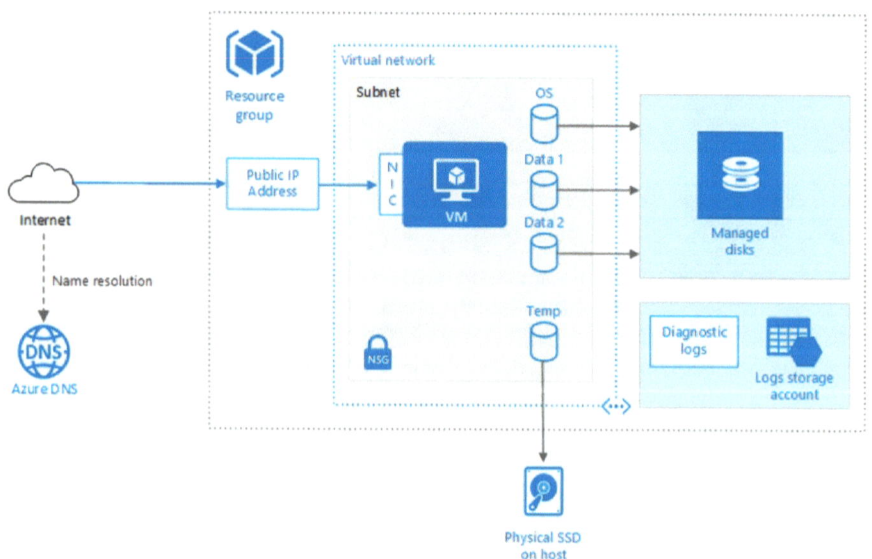

Figure: 5.1 **Virtual Machines Provisioning**

1. Types of VM Provisioning

- Static Provisioning: This traditional approach involves manually creating VMs based on predefined configurations. Administrators specify the resources needed (CPU, memory, storage) for each VM before deployment. While it provides control, it can be time-consuming and less flexible in responding to changing demands.
- Dynamic Provisioning: In this method, VMs are created automatically based on real-time demand. Automated systems can allocate resources as needed, making it easier to scale up or down without manual intervention. This approach enhances flexibility and optimizes resource utilization.
- Self-Service Provisioning: This empowers end-users or application developers to provision their own VMs through a centralized portal or dashboard. By providing predefined templates, organizations can control resource allocation while allowing users to deploy VMs quickly.

2. Provisioning Methods

- Image-Based Provisioning: This method involves using pre-configured VM images or templates that contain the operating system, applications, and settings. Images can be stored in a central repository and quickly deployed to create new VMs, significantly speeding up the provisioning process.
- Scripting and Automation: Tools like Terraform, Ansible, or PowerShell scripts can automate the provisioning process. Scripts define the desired configuration, and automation tools handle the creation, configuration, and deployment of VMs, reducing manual effort and errors.
- Cloud APIs: Major cloud providers (e.g., AWS, Azure, Google Cloud) offer APIs that enable programmatic VM provisioning. Developers can integrate these APIs into applications or workflows to dynamically create and manage VMs as needed.

3. Provisioning Tools

Various tools facilitate VM provisioning, including:

- Virtualization Platforms: Solutions like VMware vSphere, Microsoft Hyper-V, and KVM provide robust environments for creating and managing VMs, complete with templates and automation features.
- Cloud Management Platforms: Tools such as CloudBolt or RightScale provide centralized management for multi-cloud environments, allowing for streamlined provisioning and resource allocation.
- Container Orchestration: While focused on containers, tools like Kubernetes also support VM provisioning through the creation of virtualized environments for applications that require both containers and VMs.

4. Best Practices for VM Provisioning

- Use Templates: Create standardized VM templates that include the necessary configurations and applications. This simplifies the provisioning process and ensures consistency across deployments.
- Automate Where Possible: Implement automation tools to reduce manual intervention. This not only speeds up the provisioning process but also minimizes errors.
- Monitor Resource Utilization: Continuously monitor VM performance and resource usage to optimize provisioning strategies. Tools that provide real-time analytics can help identify underutilized or overutilized VMs.
- Implement Governance Policies: Establish policies for resource allocation, usage limits, and access controls to prevent resource sprawl and ensure compliance with organizational standards.
- Regular Updates and Maintenance: Keep VM images and templates up to date with the latest patches and configurations. Regularly review and optimize existing VMs to align with changing business needs.

VM provisioning is a critical process that enables organizations to deploy and manage virtual resources efficiently. By understanding the types of provisioning, utilizing effective methods and tools, and following best practices, organizations can optimize their virtualization strategies. This not only enhances operational efficiency but also supports agility and scalability in today's fast-paced IT environments. As technology continues to evolve, adopting modern provisioning techniques will be essential for leveraging the full potential of virtualization and cloud computing.

5.2 Migration Services Introduction

Migration services are essential components of modern IT strategy, facilitating the transfer of data, applications, and workloads from one environment to another. Whether transitioning to cloud platforms, upgrading systems, or consolidating data centers, effective migration services ensure minimal disruption, enhanced performance, and improved operational efficiency. This introduction outlines the significance of migration services, their types, processes, and best practices.

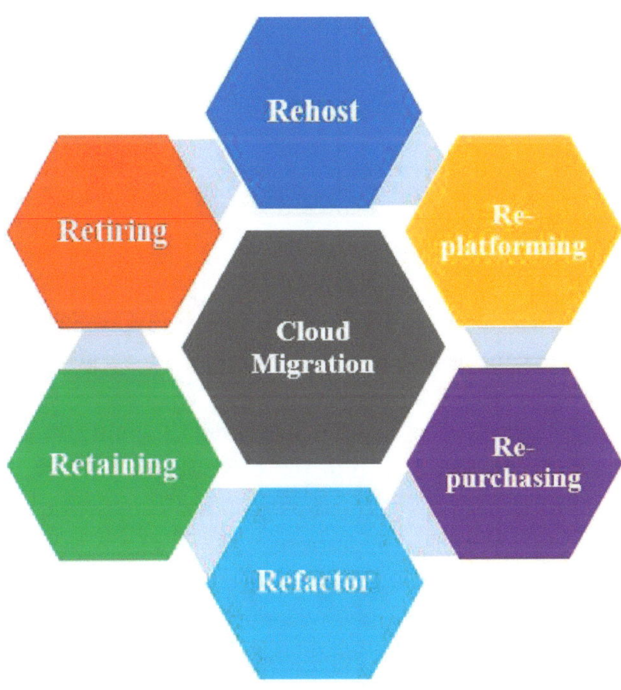

Figure: 5.2 Cloud Migration Services

1. The Importance of Migration Services

As organizations evolve, their IT environments often become fragmented or outdated. Factors driving the need for migration services include:

- Cloud Adoption: Many businesses are migrating to cloud environments to leverage scalability, flexibility, and cost efficiency. Cloud migration enables organizations to benefit from modern infrastructure without the overhead of managing physical hardware.

- System Upgrades: Upgrading to newer versions of applications or operating systems often requires migrating existing data and configurations to ensure compatibility and take advantage of enhanced features.
- Data Center Consolidation: Businesses may consolidate multiple data centers to reduce operational costs, improve resource utilization, and simplify management.
- Disaster Recovery: Effective migration strategies can enhance disaster recovery capabilities by replicating critical workloads in a separate environment, ensuring business continuity.

2. Types of Migration Services

Migration services can be categorized into several types:

- Data Migration: Involves transferring data between storage systems or formats. This may include databases, file systems, and application data, often requiring careful planning to maintain data integrity and minimize downtime.
- Application Migration: Focuses on moving applications from one environment to another, which may involve reconfiguring them to work with new infrastructure or platforms. This can include both cloud migration and on-premises migrations.
- Cloud Migration: Specifically targets the transfer of workloads from on-premises data centers to cloud environments. This can include lift-and-shift migrations (moving applications without changes) or re-architecting for cloud-native capabilities.
- Virtual Machine Migration: Involves moving VMs from one host to another, often as part of a broader strategy to optimize resources or implement disaster recovery solutions.

3. The Migration Process

The migration process typically involves several key steps:

- Assessment: Conduct a thorough assessment of the existing environment to identify applications, data, and workloads that need migration. This step includes evaluating dependencies, performance metrics, and compliance requirements.

- Planning: Develop a detailed migration plan that outlines the timeline, resources, and specific steps required for the migration. This plan should also include rollback strategies to address any potential issues.
- Execution: Implement the migration according to the established plan. This phase may involve data transfer, application reconfiguration, and testing to ensure functionality.
- Testing and Validation: After migration, conduct comprehensive testing to validate that applications and data are functioning correctly in the new environment. This step is critical for ensuring that SLAs and performance metrics are met.
- Monitoring and Optimization: Post-migration, ongoing monitoring is essential to identify any performance issues or resource constraints. Continuous optimization ensures that the new environment operates efficiently.

4. Best Practices for Successful Migrations

To ensure a successful migration, organizations should follow best practices, including:

- Involve Stakeholders: Engage key stakeholders throughout the process to ensure alignment and address concerns.
- Document Everything: Maintain thorough documentation of the entire migration process, including configurations, dependencies, and issues encountered.
- Pilot Testing: Conduct pilot migrations for critical applications or data to identify potential challenges before the full-scale migration.
- Backup Data: Always create backups of data and applications before migration to safeguard against data loss.
- Continuous Communication: Maintain open lines of communication with all parties involved to address any issues promptly and keep everyone informed of progress.

Migration services play a vital role in the transformation of IT environments, enabling organizations to adapt to changing technological landscapes. By understanding the importance, types, processes, and best practices associated with migration services, businesses can ensure seamless transitions that enhance performance, reduce risks, and support future growth. As digital transformation continues to accelerate, effective migration strategies will be key to unlocking the full potential of modern IT infrastructures.

5.3 Broad approaches to migrating into the cloud

Migrating to the cloud has become a strategic imperative for many organizations seeking to enhance agility, reduce costs, and leverage advanced technologies. The process of migration, however, can be complex and requires careful planning. Here are some broad approaches to migrating into the cloud:

1. Lift and Shift (Rehosting)

The "Lift and Shift" approach involves moving applications and workloads from on-premises data centers to the cloud with minimal modification. This method is often the quickest way to migrate, as it requires no significant changes to the application architecture. Key benefits include:

- Speed: Rapid deployment as existing applications are moved directly to the cloud.
- Lower Initial Investment: Since no major redesign is needed, costs are often lower at the outset.
- Immediate Cloud Benefits: Organizations can start leveraging cloud features like scalability and flexibility almost immediately.

However, this approach may not fully exploit the cloud's potential benefits, such as cost optimization and performance enhancements.

2. Replatforming (Lift, Tinker, and Shift)

Replatforming involves making some optimizations to applications before migrating them to the cloud. This may include updating components or taking advantage of managed services offered by cloud providers. Benefits include:

- Enhanced Performance: By optimizing the application for the cloud, organizations can achieve better performance and reliability.
- Cost Savings: Leveraging cloud-native services, like databases or load balancers, can lead to reduced operational costs.
- Minimal Disruption: Changes are generally manageable and do not require a complete overhaul of the application.

Replatforming strikes a balance between speed and optimization, allowing businesses to reap some cloud benefits without extensive re-architecting.

3. Refactoring (Rearchitecting)

Refactoring entails re-architecting applications to take full advantage of cloud-native features and services. This approach is more resource-intensive but allows organizations to optimize applications for the cloud environment. Benefits include:

- Scalability and Flexibility: Applications can be designed to dynamically scale based on demand.
- Improved Performance: Leveraging microservices architecture or serverless computing can enhance responsiveness and efficiency.
- Future-Proofing: A well-architected application is easier to update and integrate with emerging technologies.

While refactoring offers significant long-term advantages, it requires more time, effort, and investment upfront.

4. Rebuilding (Cloud-Native Development)

Rebuilding involves developing applications from scratch using cloud-native technologies. This approach is suitable for organizations with new projects or when existing applications are outdated. Key benefits include:

- Optimal Cloud Utilization: Applications are designed specifically for cloud environments, maximizing performance and efficiency.
- Enhanced Agility: Development teams can leverage modern development practices, such as DevOps, continuous integration, and continuous delivery (CI/CD).
- Innovative Capabilities: Organizations can incorporate advanced features, such as AI and machine learning, that may not be feasible with legacy systems.

Rebuilding is the most resource-intensive approach but can lead to groundbreaking applications that drive business innovation.

5. Retiring and Replacing

In some cases, organizations may find that certain applications are no longer necessary or relevant. The retiring and replacing approach involves decommissioning outdated applications and replacing them with new cloud-native solutions or services. Benefits include:

- Cost Reduction: Eliminating unused or redundant applications can reduce costs associated with maintenance and licensing.
- Streamlined Operations: Replacing legacy applications with modern solutions can simplify IT operations and enhance user experience.
- Focus on Core Business: Organizations can redirect resources to focus on strategic initiatives rather than maintaining outdated systems.

Choosing the right approach for migrating to the cloud depends on an organization's specific needs, goals, and existing infrastructure. Each approach—whether lift and shift, replatforming, refactoring, rebuilding, or retiring—offers distinct advantages and trade-offs. A well-defined migration strategy, tailored to an organization's objectives, will facilitate a smoother transition to the cloud, unlocking its full potential for innovation and efficiency. By carefully assessing applications and workloads, organizations can determine the most effective path to leverage the benefits of cloud computing.

5.4 The seven-step model of migration into a cloud

Migrating to the cloud can be a complex and challenging process, requiring careful planning and execution. A structured approach, such as the seven-step model, can help organizations navigate this journey effectively. Here's an overview of each step in the model:

1. Assessment

The first step involves a comprehensive assessment of the existing IT environment. Organizations should evaluate their current applications, data, and infrastructure to determine which components are suitable for migration. Key activities include:

- Inventory: Catalog all applications and data, noting dependencies, performance requirements, and compliance considerations.
- Cost Analysis: Estimate the total cost of ownership (TCO) for both on-premises and cloud environments, including potential savings.
- Readiness Assessment: Assess the technical readiness of applications for cloud migration, identifying any necessary modifications or upgrades.

This step provides a solid foundation for the migration strategy, highlighting potential challenges and opportunities.

2. Planning

Once the assessment is complete, the next step is to develop a detailed migration plan. This plan should outline the migration strategy, timeline, and resource allocation. Key components include:

- Migration Strategy: Decide on the appropriate migration approach for each application (e.g., lift and shift, refactoring).
- Risk Management: Identify potential risks and develop mitigation strategies.
- Stakeholder Engagement: Involve key stakeholders to ensure alignment and address any concerns.

A well-structured plan sets clear expectations and minimizes disruptions during the migration process.

3. Design

In the design phase, organizations create a blueprint for the target cloud environment. This involves:

Architecture Design: Define the architecture of the cloud environment, considering aspects such as network topology, security, and compliance requirements.

Data Management: Plan for data migration, including data formats, integrity checks, and storage solutions.

Integration: Outline how applications will integrate with existing systems and services.

This step ensures that the cloud environment will meet performance, security, and scalability needs.

4. Migration Preparation

Preparation is crucial for a successful migration. Activities during this phase include:

- Tool Selection: Identify and implement migration tools that align with the chosen strategy, such as data transfer services, orchestration tools, or APIs.
- Environment Setup: Provision the cloud environment, setting up necessary resources, security configurations, and monitoring solutions.
- Pilot Testing: Conduct pilot migrations for non-critical applications to validate the process and identify potential issues.

Thorough preparation reduces risks and ensures a smoother transition during the actual migration.

5. Migration Execution

This is the core phase where the actual migration occurs. Depending on the strategy, this may involve:

- Data Migration: Transfer data to the cloud, ensuring integrity and security throughout the process.
- Application Migration: Move applications according to the predefined strategy, whether through rehosting, refactoring, or rebuilding.
- Real-time Monitoring: Monitor the migration process to detect and address any issues as they arise.

Effective execution is critical to maintaining service continuity and performance during migration.

6. Testing and Validation

After migration, thorough testing is essential to ensure that applications and data function as expected. Activities include:

- Functional Testing: Verify that applications operate correctly in the cloud environment.
- Performance Testing: Assess the performance of applications to ensure they meet established benchmarks.
- Security Testing: Conduct security assessments to confirm compliance with organizational policies and regulations.

This step helps identify any issues that may affect user experience or operational efficiency.

7. Optimization and Continuous Improvement

The final step involves optimizing the cloud environment post-migration. This includes:

- Monitoring and Reporting: Utilize monitoring tools to track performance metrics and resource utilization.
- Cost Management: Analyze cloud expenditures and implement strategies for cost optimization.
- Continuous Improvement: Gather feedback from users and stakeholders to identify areas for further enhancement.

By focusing on optimization, organizations can ensure that their cloud environment remains efficient, secure, and aligned with business objectives.

The seven-step model of cloud migration provides a structured framework for organizations seeking to transition to cloud environments. By following these steps—assessment, planning, design, preparation, execution, testing, and optimization—businesses can minimize risks, enhance operational efficiency, and fully leverage the benefits of cloud computing. A well-executed migration strategy is essential for achieving long-term success and innovation in the digital landscape.

5.5 Virtual machines provisioning and manageability

Virtual machines (VMs) play a crucial role in modern IT environments, enabling efficient resource utilization, flexibility, and scalability. The processes of provisioning and managing VMs are vital for organizations looking to leverage virtualization and cloud computing effectively. This discussion covers the key aspects of VM provisioning and manageability, highlighting best practices and tools that facilitate these processes.

1. VM Provisioning

Provisioning refers to the creation, configuration, and deployment of virtual machines. Efficient provisioning is essential for minimizing downtime and ensuring that resources are readily available to meet business demands. There are several approaches to VM provisioning:

- Static Provisioning: In this traditional method, administrators manually create VMs based on predefined configurations. While this approach allows for detailed control over each VM's settings, it can be time-consuming and less agile in responding to fluctuating resource needs.

- Dynamic Provisioning: This method automates the creation of VMs based on real-time demand. Using orchestration tools, organizations can dynamically allocate resources, allowing for rapid scaling up or down without manual intervention. This is particularly beneficial in cloud environments where workloads can vary significantly.

- Self-Service Provisioning: Empowering users to provision their own VMs through a self-service portal can enhance efficiency. By offering predefined templates, organizations can maintain control over configurations while allowing users to deploy resources quickly.

- Image-Based Provisioning: Utilizing pre-configured VM images simplifies the deployment process. Organizations can create a master image with the required operating system, applications, and settings, which can then be quickly replicated to create new VMs.

2. VM Manageability

Once VMs are provisioned, effective manageability becomes crucial for maintaining performance, security, and compliance. Key aspects of VM manageability include:

- Monitoring and Performance Management: Continuous monitoring of VM performance metrics (such as CPU usage, memory, and disk I/O) is essential for identifying potential issues. Tools like VMware vRealize Operations, Microsoft System Center, and cloud-native monitoring solutions provide real-time insights, enabling proactive management.
- Automation and Orchestration: Automation tools (like Ansible, Puppet, or Terraform) streamline management tasks such as deployment, configuration, and updates. Orchestration platforms, like Kubernetes, facilitate the management of containerized applications alongside VMs, enhancing operational efficiency.
- Security Management: Ensuring the security of VMs is critical. This involves implementing security policies, managing access controls, and conducting regular vulnerability assessments. Solutions like firewalls, intrusion detection systems, and antivirus software should be integrated into the VM management strategy.
- Backup and Disaster Recovery: Regular backups are essential to protect data and ensure business continuity. Organizations should implement automated backup solutions that align with their recovery point objectives (RPOs) and recovery time objectives (RTOs). Additionally, disaster recovery plans should be in place to address potential outages.
- Resource Optimization: Effective management includes the continuous optimization of resource usage. Identifying underutilized or overprovisioned VMs allows organizations to reclaim resources, reducing costs and improving efficiency.

3. Best Practices for Provisioning and Manageability

To optimize VM provisioning and manageability, organizations should adopt best practices, including:

- Standardization: Use standardized templates and configurations to ensure consistency across VMs, simplifying management and reducing errors.
- Regular Audits: Conduct periodic audits of VM configurations, resource usage, and security settings to identify potential issues and ensure compliance.
- User Training: Educate users and administrators on best practices for VM provisioning and management, ensuring a clear understanding of processes and tools.

Effective provisioning and management of virtual machines are critical for organizations aiming to maximize the benefits of virtualization and cloud computing. By employing dynamic provisioning methods, robust management tools, and best practices, businesses can enhance efficiency, reduce costs, and improve service delivery. As IT environments continue to evolve, a focus on streamlined provisioning and effective manageability will remain essential for success in an increasingly digital landscape.

5.6 Virtual machine migration services

Virtual machine (VM) migration services are critical in today's IT landscape, allowing organizations to move their virtualized workloads seamlessly across different environments. Whether transitioning from on-premises infrastructure to the cloud, migrating between cloud providers, or upgrading hardware, effective VM migration ensures minimal downtime, optimal performance, and business continuity. This overview discusses the significance, types, processes, and best practices associated with VM migration services.

1. Importance of VM Migration Services

As organizations evolve, their IT infrastructures must adapt to changing business needs. The importance of VM migration services includes:

- Resource Optimization: By migrating VMs to more efficient environments, organizations can reduce costs and improve resource utilization.
- Scalability: Migrating to cloud platforms provides the ability to scale resources dynamically based on demand.
- Disaster Recovery: VM migration is vital for implementing effective disaster recovery strategies, allowing organizations to replicate VMs in remote locations.

- Upgrades and Modernization: As technology advances, migrating VMs to newer platforms or hardware can help organizations leverage improved capabilities and performance.

2. Types of VM Migration

VM migration can be categorized into several types based on the specific use case and objectives:

- Cold Migration: This involves moving VMs that are powered off. While it ensures data integrity, it requires downtime, making it suitable for less critical workloads.
- Hot Migration: Also known as live migration, this method allows VMs to be moved while they are running. This minimizes downtime and is ideal for mission-critical applications that require continuous availability.
- Cross-Cloud Migration: Organizations may need to migrate VMs between different cloud providers. This can help optimize costs or leverage specific services offered by another provider.
- On-Premises to Cloud Migration: Many organizations are migrating their on-premises VMs to cloud environments to take advantage of scalability, flexibility, and reduced management overhead.

3. Migration Process

The VM migration process typically involves several key steps:

- Assessment: Conduct a thorough analysis of the existing environment to understand the dependencies, performance metrics, and resource requirements of the VMs being migrated. This assessment is crucial for determining the best migration strategy.
- Planning: Develop a comprehensive migration plan that includes timelines, resource allocation, risk management strategies, and communication with stakeholders. This step ensures that all parties are aligned and that the migration can proceed smoothly.
- Preparation: Set up the target environment, ensuring that all necessary configurations, resources, and security measures are in place before migration. This may involve creating VM templates or images in the new environment.
- Execution: Initiate the migration, whether through cold or hot migration techniques. During this phase, it's essential to monitor the process

closely to address any issues that arise promptly.

- Testing and Validation: After migration, conduct thorough testing to ensure that applications and services are functioning correctly in the new environment. This includes performance testing, security assessments, and validation of data integrity.
- Optimization: Post-migration, organizations should continuously monitor the performance of migrated VMs, making adjustments as necessary to optimize resource utilization and enhance performance.

4. Best Practices for VM Migration

To ensure successful VM migration, organizations should follow best practices, including:

- Automate Where Possible: Use automation tools and scripts to streamline the migration process, reducing the risk of human error.
- Backup Critical Data: Always perform backups before migration to safeguard against potential data loss.
- Engage Stakeholders: Keep all relevant stakeholders informed throughout the migration process to address concerns and ensure alignment.
- Document Everything: Maintain thorough documentation of the migration process, configurations, and any issues encountered to aid in future migrations and troubleshooting.

VM migration services are essential for organizations looking to adapt their IT infrastructure to meet evolving business demands. By understanding the importance of migration, the various types available, and the steps involved in the process, businesses can effectively manage their virtual environments. Implementing best practices throughout the migration process will ensure a smooth transition, optimizing resource utilization and enhancing overall operational efficiency. As technology continues to advance, effective VM migration strategies will be key to leveraging the full benefits of virtualization and cloud computing.

5.7 VM provisioning and migration in action

VM provisioning and migration are pivotal for organizations transitioning to cloud environments. For instance, consider a company that needs to scale its operations due to increased user demand. Using dynamic provisioning, IT can automatically allocate additional VMs based on real-time metrics, ensuring resources match workload requirements without manual intervention.

Once the new VMs are provisioned, the organization may decide to migrate existing applications to the cloud for better performance. Utilizing hot migration, the IT team can move running VMs from on-premises servers to a cloud provider with minimal downtime. This process involves assessing dependencies, planning the migration strategy, and executing it while monitoring performance metrics to address any issues.

After migration, thorough testing is conducted to validate application functionality and performance in the cloud environment. Continuous optimization follows, where resource usage is monitored, and adjustments are made to ensure efficiency and cost-effectiveness.

This integrated approach to provisioning and migration not only enhances scalability but also maximizes resource utilization, enabling organizations to respond swiftly to changing business needs while maintaining high service levels.

5.8 Provisioning in the Cloud Context

Provisioning in the cloud context refers to the process of allocating and managing cloud resources, such as virtual machines (VMs), storage, and networking, to meet the demands of applications and users. This process is vital for ensuring that organizations can scale their IT resources dynamically, optimize performance, and manage costs effectively. Here's a closer look at the key aspects of cloud provisioning, its types, challenges, and best practices.

1. Types of Cloud Provisioning

Cloud provisioning can be categorized into several types based on how resources are allocated and managed:

- On-Demand Provisioning: This approach allows resources to be allocated as needed, typically through a self-service portal. Users can request resources based on immediate requirements, enabling rapid scaling without manual intervention.
- Automatic Provisioning: Leveraging automation tools and scripts, automatic provisioning enables organizations to allocate resources based on predefined rules and thresholds. For instance, when CPU usage exceeds a certain limit, additional VMs can be provisioned automatically.
- Scheduled Provisioning: In this method, resources are allocated at predetermined times. This is particularly useful for workloads with

predictable usage patterns, such as batch processing or seasonal applications, allowing organizations to optimize costs by scaling down resources during off-peak hours.

- Self-Service Provisioning: This empowers users or departments to provision their own resources through an interface or dashboard, enabling faster deployments and reducing the workload on IT teams. Organizations often set governance policies to ensure compliance and control over resource usage.

2. Provisioning Processes

The provisioning process typically involves several steps:

- Request: Users initiate requests for resources through a management interface or API, specifying their requirements such as compute power, storage, and networking.
- Validation: The system checks the request against policies and availability, ensuring compliance with organizational standards.
- Allocation: Resources are allocated based on the validated request. This can involve creating new VMs, allocating storage, or configuring network settings.
- Configuration: After allocation, resources are configured to meet the specified requirements, including installing software, setting up networking, and applying security policies.
- Monitoring: Continuous monitoring is essential for managing resource performance and utilization. Organizations can leverage monitoring tools to track metrics and optimize resource allocation dynamically.

3. Challenges in Cloud Provisioning

While cloud provisioning offers numerous benefits, it also presents challenges, including:

- Resource Management: As the number of provisioned resources increases, managing them effectively becomes complex. Organizations may face difficulties in tracking usage, costs, and performance.
- Cost Control: Without proper monitoring and management, organizations risk overspending on cloud resources. Unused or underutilized resources can lead to unexpected costs.

- Security and Compliance: Ensuring that provisioned resources comply with security policies and regulations is critical. Organizations must implement measures to secure resources from unauthorized access and vulnerabilities.
- Integration: Integrating cloud provisioning with existing on-premises infrastructure and applications can be challenging, requiring robust strategies for hybrid environments.

4. Best Practices for Cloud Provisioning

To optimize cloud provisioning, organizations should adopt the following best practices:

- Standardization: Use standardized templates for provisioning to ensure consistency, reduce errors, and streamline the process.
- Automation: Implement automation tools for provisioning and deprovisioning to enhance efficiency and reduce manual workloads.
- Monitoring and Reporting: Utilize monitoring tools to track resource utilization and performance, enabling proactive management and cost control.
- Governance Policies: Establish clear policies for resource usage, access control, and compliance to ensure that provisioning aligns with organizational standards.

Provisioning in the cloud context is a critical function that enables organizations to manage their IT resources effectively. By understanding the types of provisioning, following structured processes, addressing challenges, and implementing best practices, businesses can optimize resource utilization, enhance performance, and reduce costs. As cloud environments continue to evolve, effective provisioning strategies will remain essential for achieving operational efficiency and business agility.

5.9 Future Research Directions

As cloud computing continues to evolve, several emerging trends and challenges present opportunities for future research. Understanding these directions can help organizations leverage the cloud more effectively and address the complexities associated with its growth. Here are some key areas for future research in cloud computing:

1. Serverless Computing and Function-as-a-Service (FaaS)

Serverless computing allows developers to build and run applications without managing infrastructure, enabling a more streamlined development process. Future research can focus on improving FaaS platforms' scalability, performance, and cost-effectiveness. Investigating ways to optimize resource allocation dynamically and enhance execution speed while maintaining security and compliance will be crucial as organizations increasingly adopt this model.

2. Edge Computing Integration

As the Internet of Things (IoT) proliferates, edge computing emerges as a critical complement to cloud services. Research should explore efficient methods for integrating edge computing with cloud environments, including data processing, analytics, and storage. Investigating how to manage distributed resources effectively, ensure data consistency, and maintain security across edge and cloud infrastructures will be vital for supporting real-time applications and reducing latency.

3. Multi-Cloud and Hybrid Cloud Strategies

Organizations are increasingly adopting multi-cloud and hybrid cloud environments to avoid vendor lock-in and optimize costs. Future research should focus on developing strategies and frameworks for managing these complex environments. This includes investigating interoperability standards, workload migration techniques, and unified management tools to simplify operations across multiple cloud platforms while ensuring compliance and security.

4. Security and Privacy Enhancements

As cloud adoption grows, so do concerns about security and privacy. Research in this area should focus on advanced security frameworks, including the development of more sophisticated encryption methods, identity and access management solutions, and anomaly detection systems. Additionally, exploring privacy-preserving techniques, such as federated learning and secure multi-party computation, can help organizations leverage cloud resources while maintaining data confidentiality.

5. Artificial Intelligence and Machine Learning Integration

Integrating AI and machine learning into cloud services can enhance resource management, automate processes, and improve decision-making. Future research should explore how AI can optimize resource allocation, predict workload patterns, and automate deployment processes. Additionally, investigating AI-driven security solutions can help identify vulnerabilities and enhance threat detection capabilities.

6. Sustainability and Green Cloud Computing

As environmental concerns rise, research into sustainable cloud computing practices becomes increasingly important. Future studies should focus on reducing the carbon footprint of data centers, optimizing energy consumption, and exploring renewable energy sources. Additionally, investigating frameworks for assessing and improving the sustainability of cloud services will be crucial for organizations aiming to meet regulatory requirements and corporate social responsibility goals.

7. User Experience and Service Level Agreements (SLAs)

Improving the user experience in cloud services is essential for user satisfaction and retention. Research can delve into user-centric design principles, optimizing interfaces, and enhancing accessibility. Furthermore, developing frameworks for defining and enforcing SLAs that are clear, measurable, and adaptable to changing business needs will be vital in ensuring service quality and reliability.

The future of cloud computing holds significant potential for innovation and improvement. By focusing on these research directions—serverless computing, edge integration, multi-cloud strategies, security enhancements, AI integration, sustainability, and user experience—researchers and practitioners can address the challenges facing cloud environments and drive the next wave of advancements. Embracing these opportunities will enable organizations to maximize the benefits of cloud computing while navigating its complexities.

CHAPTER SIX

Management of Virtual Machines for Cloud Infrastructures

6.1 Management of Virtual Machines for Cloud Infrastructures

Effective management of virtual machines (VMs) is crucial for the success of cloud infrastructures. As organizations increasingly rely on cloud environments to host applications and services, efficient VM management ensures optimal performance, resource utilization, and cost-effectiveness. Here's an overview of key strategies and practices for managing VMs in cloud infrastructures.

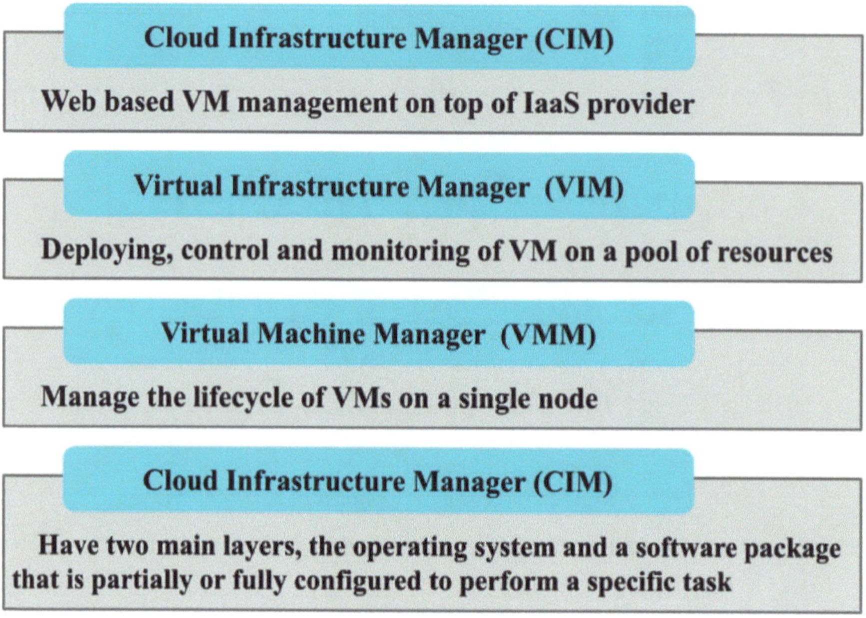

Cloud Infrastructure Manager (CIM)

Web based VM management on top of IaaS provider

Virtual Infrastructure Manager (VIM)

Deploying, control and monitoring of VM on a pool of resources

Virtual Machine Manager (VMM)

Manage the lifecycle of VMs on a single node

Cloud Infrastructure Manager (CIM)

Have two main layers, the operating system and a software package that is partially or fully configured to perform a specific task

Figure 6.1: VM management layers of a cloud infrastructure platform

1. Provisioning and Deployment

The first step in VM management is provisioning and deploying virtual machines. Cloud providers often offer automated tools and dashboards to simplify this process. Users can select the desired configuration, including CPU, memory, storage, and operating system, and deploy VMs quickly. Infrastructure as Code (IaC) tools, such as Terraform or AWS CloudFormation, enable organizations to automate and version-control the deployment of VMs, ensuring consistency across environments.

2. Resource Monitoring and Optimization

Continuous monitoring of VM performance is vital to ensure that resources are being used effectively. Cloud management platforms often provide real-time analytics on CPU usage, memory consumption, disk I/O, and network traffic. By analyzing these metrics, organizations can identify underutilized or overutilized VMs.

Dynamic scaling, or autoscaling, can be employed to automatically adjust the number of VMs based on demand, ensuring that resources align with workload requirements. This not only optimizes performance but also reduces costs by minimizing idle resources.

3. Lifecycle Management

VMs go through various stages, including provisioning, operation, maintenance, and decommissioning. Lifecycle management involves maintaining VMs throughout their lifecycle to ensure optimal performance and security. Regular updates and patches must be applied to the operating system and applications running on VMs to protect against vulnerabilities.

Additionally, organizations should establish policies for VM retirement. VMs that are no longer in use can be decommissioned to free up resources and reduce costs. Automated tools can help schedule regular audits to identify and clean up unused VMs.

4. Security and Compliance

Security is a critical aspect of VM management in cloud infrastructures. Each VM must be secured with appropriate firewalls, intrusion detection systems, and access controls. Implementing role-based access control (RBAC) helps ensure that only authorized personnel can access specific VMs.

Data encryption, both at rest and in transit, is essential for protecting sensitive information. Regular security assessments and compliance checks help organizations adhere to industry standards and regulatory requirements, such as GDPR or HIPAA.

5. Backup and Disaster Recovery

Regular backups are essential for protecting data and ensuring business continuity in case of failures or disasters. VM snapshots allow administrators to capture the state of a VM at a specific point in time, enabling quick recovery. Organizations should implement a disaster recovery plan that outlines procedures for restoring VMs and data in the event of a failure.

Cloud providers typically offer integrated backup and disaster recovery solutions, allowing organizations to automate these processes and ensure minimal downtime.

6. Cost Management

Managing costs in cloud environments is critical, as expenses can escalate quickly. Organizations should regularly review their VM usage and associated costs, leveraging cloud cost management tools to track and analyze spending.

Implementing tagging strategies helps categorize VMs based on projects or departments, providing better visibility into resource allocation and costs. Setting budget alerts can help organizations stay within their spending limits.

The management of virtual machines in cloud infrastructures is a multifaceted process that requires careful planning and execution. By focusing on provisioning, monitoring, lifecycle management, security, backup, and cost management, organizations can optimize their cloud environments to deliver robust, efficient, and secure services. As cloud technology continues to evolve, staying informed about best practices and emerging tools will be essential for effective VM management and maximizing the benefits of cloud computing.

6.2 The Anatomy of Cloud Infrastructures

Cloud infrastructure forms the backbone of modern computing, providing scalable and flexible resources that can be accessed over the internet. Understanding its anatomy is essential for businesses looking to leverage cloud services effectively. Here's a breakdown of the key components of cloud infrastructures.

1. Physical Layer

At the base of cloud infrastructure lies the physical layer, consisting of data centers equipped with hardware such as servers, storage devices, and networking equipment. These data centers are strategically located in various geographic regions to ensure redundancy and minimize latency. The physical infrastructure is crucial for hosting virtualized resources and maintaining high availability.

2. Virtualization Layer

Above the physical layer is the virtualization layer, where hypervisors play a vital role. Hypervisors, such as VMware ESXi, Microsoft Hyper-V, and KVM, abstract physical resources and enable the creation of virtual machines (VMs). This layer allows multiple VMs to share the same physical hardware, enhancing resource utilization and flexibility.

Virtualization also includes technologies for containerization (e.g., Docker, Kubernetes), which package applications and their dependencies into lightweight containers, facilitating efficient deployment and scaling.

3. Storage Layer

The storage layer is responsible for managing data in cloud infrastructures. This includes:

- Block Storage: Provides raw storage volumes that can be attached to VMs, ideal for databases and transactional applications.

- Object Storage: Stores data as objects, suitable for unstructured data like media files and backups. Services like Amazon S3 exemplify this type.
- File Storage: Offers a file system interface, enabling users to access data as files. This is useful for applications requiring shared file access.

Efficient storage solutions ensure data durability, availability, and quick access.

4. Network Layer

The network layer connects various components of the cloud infrastructure. It includes both physical networking hardware (routers, switches) and virtual networking solutions that manage data flow between VMs, storage, and external clients. Key elements include:

- Virtual Private Networks (VPNs): Secure connections that allow users to access cloud resources safely.
- Load Balancers: Distribute incoming traffic across multiple VMs to ensure optimal performance and availability.
- Firewalls: Protect cloud resources by monitoring and controlling incoming and outgoing network traffic.

This layer is crucial for ensuring reliable and secure communication within the cloud environment.

5. Management Layer

The management layer encompasses tools and interfaces used to oversee cloud resources. This includes.

- Cloud Management Platforms (CMPs): Provide a unified interface for managing cloud resources, automating tasks, and monitoring performance. Examples include AWS Management Console and Azure Portal.
- Orchestration Tools: Automate the deployment and management of applications and services, ensuring efficient resource allocation. Tools like Kubernetes and OpenShift fall into this category.
- Monitoring and Analytics: Tools that track resource usage, performance metrics, and security events, helping organizations optimize their cloud environments.

6. Service Layer

The service layer is where various cloud services are offered to end-users, typically categorized into:

- Infrastructure as a Service (IaaS): Provides virtualized computing resources over the internet, such as VMs and storage (e.g., AWS EC2, Google Compute Engine).
- Platform as a Service (PaaS): Offers a platform for developers to build, deploy, and manage applications without managing underlying infrastructure (e.g., Heroku, Google App Engine).
- Software as a Service (SaaS): Delivers software applications over the internet, accessible via web browsers (e.g., Google Workspace, Salesforce).

This layer directly interacts with end-users, providing the services they require.

The anatomy of cloud infrastructures consists of interconnected layers—physical, virtualization, storage, network, management, and service. Each layer plays a vital role in ensuring that cloud services are efficient, reliable, and scalable. Understanding these components helps organizations make informed decisions about adopting cloud technologies and optimizing their cloud strategies for enhanced performance and innovation. As the cloud landscape continues to evolve, a solid grasp of its anatomy will be essential for leveraging its full potential.

6.3 Distributed Management of Virtual Infrastructures

Distributed management of virtual infrastructures is essential for optimizing resource utilization, ensuring high availability, and maintaining performance across geographically dispersed environments. As organizations increasingly adopt virtualization and cloud computing, effective management practices become critical to harnessing the full potential of their virtual resources. Here's a closer look at the principles, challenges, and best practices associated with distributed management.

1. Understanding Distributed Management

Distributed management refers to the approach of overseeing and controlling resources and services across multiple locations or data centers. In virtual infrastructures, this includes managing virtual machines (VMs), storage, networking, and applications that may reside in different physical or cloud environments. A distributed management system allows administrators to monitor and control these resources from a centralized interface, promoting efficiency and streamlined operations.

2. Key Components

- Centralized Management Tools: Solutions like VMware vCenter, Microsoft System Center, and cloud-native tools (e.g., AWS Management Console) provide centralized dashboards for monitoring and managing resources across various locations. These tools offer visibility into performance metrics, resource utilization, and security events.
- Automation and Orchestration: Automation tools (e.g., Ansible, Puppet) facilitate the provisioning and configuration of resources, reducing manual tasks and minimizing human error. Orchestration platforms like Kubernetes enable automated deployment, scaling, and management of containerized applications, ensuring consistent operation across distributed environments.
- Monitoring and Analytics: Advanced monitoring tools collect data on performance, availability, and resource consumption. Solutions like Prometheus and Grafana provide insights that help administrators make informed decisions about resource allocation and scaling.

3. Benefits of Distributed Management

- Scalability: Distributed management systems enable organizations to scale their virtual resources efficiently, adding or removing VMs and other services based on demand without significant downtime.
- High Availability: By managing resources across multiple locations, organizations can implement redundancy and failover mechanisms. If one data center experiences issues, services can be redirected to another location, ensuring business continuity.
- Resource Optimization: Centralized visibility into resource usage allows for better planning and allocation, helping organizations maximize their investment in infrastructure.
- Improved Performance: By distributing workloads across various geographic locations, organizations can reduce latency and improve response times for end-users, enhancing overall performance.

4. Challenges

While distributed management offers numerous advantages, it also presents challenges:

- Complexity: Managing resources across multiple locations can become complex, requiring sophisticated tools and skilled personnel to maintain oversight.
- Security Concerns: A distributed environment increases the attack surface for potential security threats. Ensuring consistent security policies and practices across locations is essential.
- Interoperability: Different virtualization technologies and cloud providers may have varying management interfaces and capabilities, complicating integration and management.
- Network Dependency: Effective distributed management relies heavily on network connectivity. Latency or outages can disrupt management tasks and impact performance.

5. Best Practices

To address these challenges, organizations should adopt best practices:

- Standardization: Implement standardized processes and tools across all virtual environments to simplify management and reduce complexity.
- Comprehensive Security Policies: Develop and enforce security protocols that are consistent across all locations, incorporating encryption, access control, and regular audits.
- Regular Training: Invest in ongoing training for IT staff to ensure they are equipped with the latest knowledge and skills to manage distributed environments effectively.
- Utilize APIs: Leverage application programming interfaces (APIs) provided by cloud providers and virtualization platforms to integrate and automate management tasks seamlessly.

Distributed management of virtual infrastructures is essential for organizations that operate in diverse and dynamic environments. By leveraging centralized management tools, automation, and advanced monitoring, businesses can enhance scalability, performance, and resilience. While challenges exist, adopting best practices can help organizations navigate the complexities of distributed management, ensuring efficient and secure operation of their virtual resources. As technology continues to evolve, effective management strategies will be crucial for maintaining competitiveness in a rapidly changing landscape.

6.4 Scheduling Techniques for Advance Reservation of Capacity

Advance reservation of capacity in cloud and distributed environments ensures that resources are allocated efficiently for future tasks, minimizing conflicts and maximizing utilization. Several scheduling techniques are employed to facilitate this process:

- Time-Slot Reservation: This technique involves dividing time into discrete slots that can be reserved in advance. Users specify the desired start time and duration, allowing the system to allocate resources accordingly. This method is straightforward but may lead to underutilization if slots remain unfilled.
- Priority-Based Scheduling: In this approach, reservations are prioritized based on user needs or application importance. High-priority tasks are allocated resources first, ensuring that critical applications receive the capacity they require. This technique can help balance resource allocation across competing demands.
- Flexible Reservations: This method allows users to specify a range of acceptable start times and durations. The scheduling system then optimizes resource allocation by filling gaps in usage patterns, improving overall utilization.
- Dynamic Capacity Allocation: Advanced algorithms dynamically adjust reservations based on real-time demand and usage patterns. Machine learning techniques can predict usage trends and optimize capacity allocation accordingly.
- Resource Pooling: By aggregating resources across multiple users or applications, this technique enhances flexibility in reservations. Resources can be shared among users, reducing the likelihood of idle capacity.

These scheduling techniques collectively enhance the efficiency of advance reservation systems, ensuring that cloud and distributed resources are optimally utilized while meeting user demands.

6.5 Capacity Management to meet SLA Commitments

Capacity management is crucial for ensuring that IT services can meet Service Level Agreement (SLA) commitments, which define the expected service performance and availability standards. Effective capacity management involves several key strategies:

- Resource Monitoring and Analysis: Continuous monitoring of resource utilization—such as CPU, memory, storage, and network bandwidth—is essential. Tools like performance analytics and dashboards provide insights into current usage patterns, helping identify potential bottlenecks.
- Forecasting Demand: Using historical data and trend analysis, organizations can predict future resource needs. This forecasting helps in proactive planning and ensures that sufficient capacity is available to handle anticipated workloads.
- Scaling Strategies: Implementing scaling techniques—both vertical (adding resources to existing servers) and horizontal (adding more servers)—allows organizations to adjust capacity dynamically based on real-time demand. This ensures that resources align with workload fluctuations.
- Performance Testing: Regular testing of applications under simulated load conditions can help identify performance limitations and areas needing enhancement. This allows organizations to proactively address issues before they impact SLAs.
- Regular Reviews and Adjustments: Periodic reviews of capacity management practices ensure they align with evolving business requirements and SLAs. Adjusting strategies based on performance metrics and changing demands fosters continuous improvement.

By implementing these strategies, organizations can effectively manage capacity, ensuring they meet SLA commitments and deliver consistent, reliable services to users. This not only enhances customer satisfaction but also supports business continuity and operational efficiency.

CHAPTER SEVEN

Cloud Security

7.1 Cloud security risks

Cloud security is a critical concern for organizations migrating to cloud computing environments. While the cloud offers numerous benefits, such as scalability and cost efficiency, it also introduces a variety of security risks that organizations must address to protect sensitive data and maintain compliance.

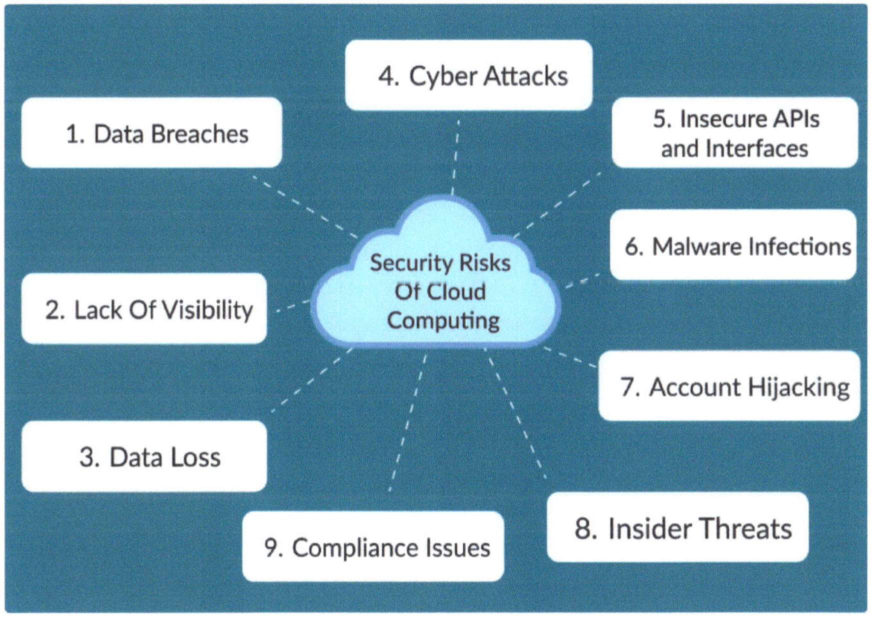

Figure 7.1: Security Risks of Cloud Computing

Key Cloud Security Risks

- Data Breaches: One of the most significant risks is the potential for unauthorized access to sensitive data. Data breaches can result from weak access controls, misconfigured cloud settings, or vulnerabilities in applications. Cybercriminals often target cloud environments to exploit these weaknesses.
- Insider Threats: Employees or contractors with access to cloud resources can pose significant risks. Insider threats can be malicious, involving intentional data theft or sabotage, or unintentional, stemming from negligence or lack of awareness about security practices.
- Insecure APIs: Many cloud services rely on APIs (Application Programming Interfaces) for interaction and integration. Insecure APIs can expose vulnerabilities that attackers can exploit to gain unauthorized access to cloud resources or sensitive data.
- Data Loss: Data can be lost due to accidental deletion, corruption, or failure of the cloud service provider. While many providers offer backup solutions, organizations must implement their own data protection strategies to mitigate this risk.
- Compliance Violations: Organizations must adhere to various regulations and standards, such as GDPR, HIPAA, or PCI DSS. Non-compliance can lead to severe penalties and reputational damage. Cloud providers may not always meet these compliance requirements, placing the onus on organizations to ensure adherence.
- Account Hijacking: Cybercriminals may attempt to gain access to user accounts through phishing attacks, weak passwords, or credential stuffing. Once an account is compromised, attackers can manipulate resources, steal data, or launch further attacks.
- Denial of Service (DoS) Attacks: Cloud services can be targeted by DoS attacks, which overwhelm the infrastructure with traffic, rendering services unavailable to legitimate users. Such attacks can disrupt operations and lead to financial losses.

Strategies for Enhancing Cloud Security

To mitigate these risks, organizations should adopt a multi-layered security approach:

- Data Encryption: Encrypting data both at rest and in transit is crucial for protecting sensitive information. This ensures that even if data is intercepted or accessed without authorization, it remains unreadable.

- Access Control and Identity Management: Implement strong access control policies, using role-based access controls (RBAC) to ensure users have only the permissions necessary for their roles. Multi-factor authentication (MFA) can further enhance security by adding an extra layer of verification.
- Regular Security Audits: Conduct regular security assessments and audits to identify vulnerabilities and ensure compliance with security policies and regulations. This proactive approach helps organizations stay ahead of potential threats.
- Security Training and Awareness: Educate employees about security best practices, phishing attacks, and the importance of following security protocols. A well-informed workforce is a critical line of defense against insider threats and social engineering attacks.
- Monitoring and Incident Response: Implement continuous monitoring to detect suspicious activities or anomalies within the cloud environment. Establish an incident response plan to ensure a swift and effective response to any security breaches or incidents.
- Choose Reputable Providers: When selecting a cloud service provider, consider their security measures, compliance certifications, and track record. Ensure they offer robust security features and support for industry standards.

7.2 The top concern for cloud users

The rapid adoption of cloud computing has transformed how organizations operate, enabling them to scale resources, enhance collaboration, and drive innovation. However, with these advantages come significant concerns, with data security emerging as the top concern for cloud users.

The Importance of Data Security

Data security encompasses the practices and technologies used to protect sensitive information from unauthorized access, theft, or loss. For cloud users, this concern is magnified due to the nature of cloud environments, where data is often stored off-site and managed by third-party providers. This shift from traditional on-premises systems to cloud-based storage raises various issues related to data integrity, confidentiality, and compliance.

Key Factors Driving Security Concerns

- Increased Vulnerability to Cyberattacks: As more organizations migrate to the cloud, cybercriminals are increasingly targeting these environments. The proliferation of data breaches highlights the vulnerabilities inherent in cloud systems. Attackers often exploit weak access controls, misconfigured settings, or insecure APIs to gain unauthorized access.

- Shared Responsibility Model: Cloud security operates on a shared responsibility model, meaning that both the cloud provider and the user have roles in ensuring security. While providers typically secure the infrastructure, users must manage data protection, access controls, and compliance. Misunderstandings about this division of responsibility can lead to security gaps.

- Insider Threats: Organizations must be vigilant against insider threats, which can be both malicious and unintentional. Employees with access to sensitive data may inadvertently expose information through negligence or phishing attacks. Malicious insiders may exploit their access for personal gain, making robust internal security measures essential.

- Compliance and Regulatory Challenges: Many industries are subject to strict regulations regarding data privacy and security, such as GDPR, HIPAA, and PCI DSS. Ensuring compliance can be challenging in a cloud environment, where data is often stored in multiple locations and jurisdictions. Non-compliance can result in hefty fines and reputational damage.

- Data Loss and Recovery Concerns: Cloud users often worry about data loss due to accidental deletion, hardware failures, or service provider outages. While many cloud providers offer backup and recovery solutions, organizations must ensure they have robust strategies in place to protect against data loss.

Mitigating Security Concerns

To address these concerns, organizations can implement several strategies:

- Data Encryption: Encrypting data both at rest and in transit is vital for safeguarding sensitive information. This ensures that even if data is intercepted, it remains unreadable to unauthorized users.

- Strong Access Controls: Organizations should implement strict access controls using role-based access management (RBAC) to ensure that only authorized personnel can access sensitive data. Multi-factor authentication (MFA) adds an additional layer of security, making it more difficult for unauthorized users to gain access.
- Regular Security Audits: Conducting regular security assessments and audits helps identify vulnerabilities and ensure compliance with internal and external security policies. This proactive approach allows organizations to stay ahead of potential threats.
- Employee Training: Providing ongoing security training for employees is essential. Awareness programs can help staff recognize phishing attempts and understand the importance of adhering to security protocols.
- Choosing Reputable Providers: When selecting a cloud service provider, organizations should evaluate their security practices, certifications, and track record. A reputable provider will offer robust security features and support for compliance with industry standards.

7.3 Privacy and privacy impact assessment

Privacy is a fundamental human right that pertains to an individual's ability to control their personal information and how it is collected, used, and shared. In the digital age, privacy has become increasingly complex due to the vast amounts of personal data being processed by organizations. This data can include anything from contact information and financial records to behavioral data gathered through online interactions. The challenge lies in balancing the need for data collection—often vital for business operations and innovation—with the rights of individuals to protect their personal information.

Importance of Privacy

The importance of privacy is underscored by the growing number of data breaches and misuse of personal information. These incidents not only harm individuals but can also damage an organization's reputation and lead to significant financial penalties. Furthermore, privacy is linked to trust; consumers are more likely to engage with organizations that demonstrate a commitment to protecting their personal data.

Privacy Regulations

As concerns about privacy have intensified, many countries have enacted regulations to safeguard personal data. Notable examples include the General Data Protection Regulation (GDPR) in the European Union and the California Consumer Privacy Act (CCPA) in the United States. These laws impose strict guidelines on how organizations must handle personal data, including requirements for transparency, consent, and data security.

What is a Privacy Impact Assessment (PIA)?

A Privacy Impact Assessment (PIA) is a systematic process used to evaluate how a project or initiative impacts the privacy of individuals. Conducting a PIA helps organizations identify potential privacy risks associated with data collection and processing, allowing them to implement measures to mitigate these risks.

Key Components of a PIA

- Project Description: Clearly define the project's purpose, scope, and the types of personal data involved.
- Stakeholder Consultation: Engage relevant stakeholders, including data subjects, legal experts, and IT personnel, to gather insights and concerns regarding privacy.
- Risk Assessment: Identify and evaluate potential privacy risks, considering both the likelihood of occurrence and the potential impact on individuals.
- Mitigation Strategies: Develop strategies to minimize identified risks, such as implementing data encryption, access controls, and anonymization techniques.
- Documentation: Document the entire PIA process, including findings and decisions made, which serves as evidence of compliance and a reference for future assessments.
- Ongoing Review: Regularly review and update the PIA as the project evolves or as new regulations emerge to ensure ongoing compliance and risk management.

Benefits of Conducting a PIA

- Enhanced Risk Management: A PIA enables organizations to proactively identify and address privacy risks, reducing the likelihood of data breaches.
- Regulatory Compliance: Completing a PIA can help organizations meet legal obligations under privacy regulations, minimizing the risk of fines and legal challenges.

- Building Trust: Demonstrating a commitment to privacy through thorough assessments fosters trust with customers and stakeholders, enhancing organizational reputation.
- Informed Decision-Making: The insights gained from a PIA can inform strategic decisions, guiding organizations on whether to proceed with, modify, or halt projects based on privacy considerations.

7.4 Trust, Operating system security

Trust in operating systems (OS) is fundamental to ensuring the security and integrity of computing environments. Operating systems serve as the backbone of computer systems, managing hardware resources and providing a platform for applications to run. The security of an OS is critical because vulnerabilities can be exploited by malicious actors, leading to unauthorized access, data breaches, and other security incidents.

The Role of Trust in OS Security

Trust in an operating system stems from its ability to provide a secure environment for users and applications. This trust is built on several foundational principles:

- Confidentiality: The OS must protect sensitive information from unauthorized access. Mechanisms like user authentication, file permissions, and encryption play essential roles in maintaining confidentiality.
- Integrity: The OS should ensure that data remains unaltered unless authorized. Integrity checks, such as checksums and digital signatures, help verify that files and data have not been tampered with.
- Availability: An OS must ensure that systems and data are accessible when needed. Security measures, including redundancy and denial-of-service protection, help maintain availability.

Key Security Features of Operating Systems

- User Authentication: Robust authentication mechanisms, such as passwords, biometrics, and two-factor authentication (2FA), ensure that only authorized users can access the system.
- Access Control: Operating systems implement access control lists (ACLs) and role-based access control (RBAC) to manage permissions. These systems determine who can access specific resources, helping to

prevent unauthorized actions.

- Sandboxing: This technique isolates applications from one another and from the OS itself. By limiting an application's access to system resources, sandboxing helps contain potential security breaches.
- Regular Updates and Patch Management: Keeping an OS up to date is crucial for security. Regular updates patch vulnerabilities, protect against new threats, and enhance overall system security.
- Malware Protection: Operating systems often come with built-in antivirus and anti-malware tools that scan for and mitigate malicious software, helping to safeguard the system from threats.

Building Trust through Security Standards

To establish trust in operating systems, adherence to security standards and best practices is vital. Standards such as ISO/IEC 27001 and the Common Criteria for Information Technology Security Evaluation provide frameworks for assessing the security capabilities of operating systems. Compliance with these standards helps organizations evaluate the trustworthiness of their OS.

The Importance of Transparency

Transparency is another key aspect of building trust in operating system security. Users and organizations need to understand how their OS handles data and security. Open-source operating systems, for example, allow users to review and audit the source code for vulnerabilities, fostering a higher level of trust compared to proprietary systems.

Challenges to Trust

Despite the measures in place, several challenges can undermine trust in operating systems:

- Complexity: As operating systems become more complex, the potential for security vulnerabilities increases. A single vulnerability can lead to widespread exploitation if not addressed promptly.
- Human Error: Users often inadvertently compromise security by using weak passwords or failing to install updates. User education and awareness are crucial for maintaining security.
- Advanced Threats: Cybercriminals continually develop new techniques to exploit OS vulnerabilities. Staying ahead of these threats requires continuous monitoring and rapid response strategies.

Trust in operating system security is essential for protecting sensitive data and maintaining the integrity of computing environments. By implementing robust security features, adhering to standards, and promoting transparency, organizations can foster trust in their operating systems. As the digital landscape evolves, maintaining this trust will require ongoing vigilance and adaptation to emerging threats, ensuring that users can rely on their operating systems for secure operations.

7.5 Virtual machine Security

As organizations increasingly adopt virtualization technologies to optimize resource utilization and enhance operational efficiency, the security of virtual machines (VMs) has become a critical concern. Virtual machines allow multiple operating systems to run on a single physical server, but they also introduce unique security challenges that must be addressed to safeguard data and maintain system integrity.

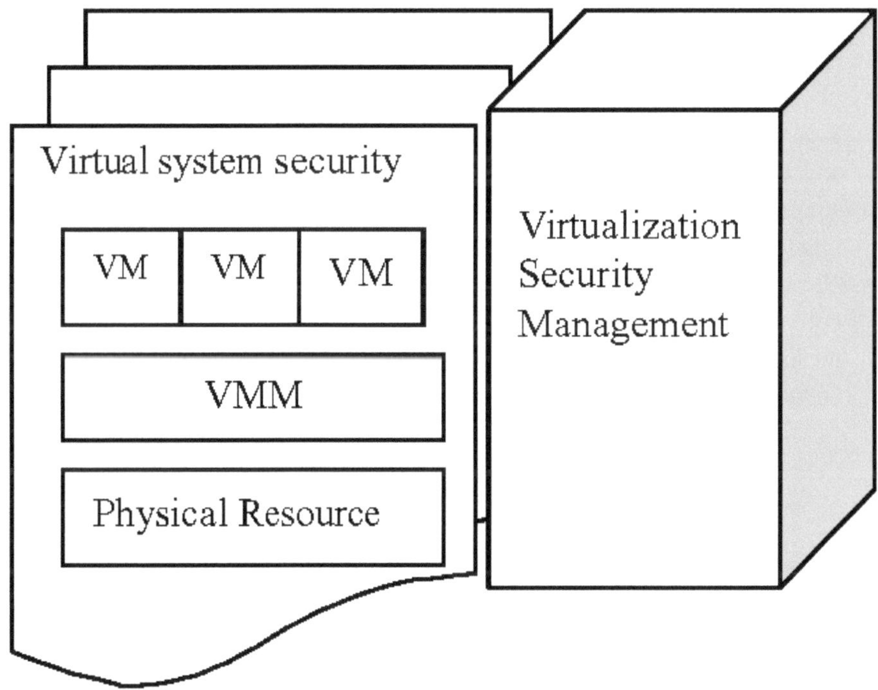

Figure 7.2: Virtual Machine Security

Understanding Virtual Machines

A virtual machine is an emulation of a physical computer, complete with its own operating system, applications, and virtual hardware. VMs are hosted on hypervisors, which manage the allocation of physical resources like CPU, memory, and storage. This abstraction layer enables improved flexibility and scalability but can also create vulnerabilities if not properly secured.

Key Security Challenges

- Hypervisor Vulnerabilities: The hypervisor is a key component in virtualization architecture. Any vulnerabilities within the hypervisor can lead to the exploitation of all VMs it manages. Attackers can potentially escape a VM to gain access to the host system or other VMs, compromising the security of the entire environment.
- Inadequate Isolation: While VMs are designed to be isolated from one another, misconfigurations or flaws can lead to breaches of this isolation. An attacker exploiting one VM could potentially access data or resources in another VM on the same host if proper security measures are not in place.
- Snapshot and Backup Security: VMs can be quickly cloned, snapshotted, and backed up, but these processes can also expose sensitive data. If snapshots or backups are not securely stored, they can be accessed by unauthorized users, leading to data leaks.
- Network Security Risks: Virtual networks are often created to allow communication between VMs. However, inadequate network security measures can expose VMs to attacks such as man-in-the-middle (MitM) and denial-of-service (DoS) attacks.

Best Practices for Securing Virtual Machines

- Secure the Hypervisor: Implement robust security measures for the hypervisor, including regular updates, strong authentication, and access controls. Limiting access to the hypervisor to only authorized personnel is crucial for protecting the entire virtualization environment.
- Network Segmentation: Use network segmentation to isolate VMs based on their roles and security requirements. This approach minimizes the risk of lateral movement by attackers and helps contain potential breaches.

- Regular Updates and Patch Management: Keep both the hypervisor and guest operating systems updated with the latest security patches. Regular maintenance is essential for mitigating vulnerabilities that could be exploited by attackers.
- Strong Access Controls: Implement strict access controls for both VMs and the hypervisor management interfaces. Use role-based access controls (RBAC) to ensure that users have the minimum level of access necessary for their roles.
- Encryption: Encrypt data both in transit and at rest to protect sensitive information stored within VMs. This ensures that even if data is intercepted or accessed by unauthorized users, it remains unreadable.
- Monitor and Audit: Continuously monitor the virtualization environment for suspicious activity and conduct regular security audits. Implementing logging and alerting mechanisms can help detect potential security incidents early.
- Secure Backups and Snapshots: Ensure that backups and snapshots are stored securely and encrypted. Access to these resources should be restricted to authorized personnel only.

Securing virtual machines is vital for protecting sensitive data and maintaining the integrity of IT environments. While virtualization offers numerous benefits, it also introduces specific security challenges that organizations must address. By implementing best practices and adopting a proactive security posture, organizations can enhance their VM security and reduce the risk of data breaches and other security incidents. In a world increasingly reliant on virtualization, investing in VM security is essential for safeguarding organizational assets and maintaining trust with clients and stakeholders.

7.6 Security of virtualization

As businesses increasingly adopt virtualization technologies to enhance efficiency and optimize resource utilization, ensuring the security of virtualization environments has become paramount. Virtualization allows multiple virtual machines (VMs) to run on a single physical host, providing benefits such as improved scalability and flexibility. However, this technology also introduces unique security challenges that must be addressed to safeguard data and maintain operational integrity.

Key Security Challenges in Virtualization

- Hypervisor Vulnerabilities: The hypervisor, which manages the creation and operation of VMs, is a critical component of virtualization. If vulnerabilities in the hypervisor are exploited, attackers can potentially gain access to all VMs on the host. Such hypervisor-level attacks can lead to data breaches and unauthorized access to sensitive information.
- Isolation Failures: While VMs are designed to be isolated from one another, misconfigurations or inherent flaws can undermine this isolation. An attacker who compromises one VM might exploit weaknesses to access data or resources in other VMs on the same host. Ensuring robust isolation is essential for preventing lateral movement within the environment.
- Insecure Interfaces and APIs: Management interfaces and APIs used to control virtual environments can be prime targets for attackers. Weak authentication and inadequate access controls can allow unauthorized users to manipulate VMs, leading to data breaches or service disruptions.
- Snapshot and Backup Risks: Virtualization technologies often allow quick snapshots and backups of VMs. However, if these backups are not adequately secured, they can expose sensitive data to unauthorized access. Protecting these resources is crucial for maintaining data confidentiality.
- Network Security Threats: Virtual networks facilitate communication between VMs, but they can also introduce vulnerabilities. Poorly configured virtual networks can expose VMs to network-based attacks, including man-in-the-middle (MitM) attacks and denial-of-service (DoS) attacks.

Best Practices for Securing Virtualization

- Strengthen Hypervisor Security: Protect the hypervisor with strong authentication mechanisms and limit access to authorized personnel only. Regularly update the hypervisor to patch known vulnerabilities and strengthen its security posture.
- Implement Strict Access Controls: Use role-based access control (RBAC) to restrict permissions based on user roles. Limit access to management interfaces and ensure that only necessary personnel can modify VM settings or access sensitive data.
- Network Segmentation: Utilize network segmentation to isolate VMs based on their functions and security requirements. By segmenting

networks, organizations can minimize the risk of lateral movement by attackers and contain potential breaches.

- Regular Monitoring and Auditing: Continuously monitor the virtualization environment for suspicious activity. Implement logging and alerting mechanisms to detect potential security incidents early. Conduct regular audits to assess compliance with security policies.
- Data Encryption: Encrypt sensitive data both at rest and in transit. This adds an additional layer of protection, ensuring that even if data is intercepted or accessed, it remains unreadable to unauthorized users.
- Secure Snapshots and Backups: Store snapshots and backups securely, using encryption and strong access controls. Ensure that backup policies are regularly reviewed to maintain data integrity and confidentiality.
- User Education and Awareness: Foster a culture of security within the organization by training users on best practices for virtualization security. Employees should be aware of potential threats and understand their role in maintaining security.

Securing virtualization environments is essential for protecting sensitive data and maintaining the overall integrity of IT operations. While virtualization offers significant advantages, it also presents unique security challenges that organizations must proactively address. By implementing best practices and adopting a comprehensive security strategy, organizations can enhance their virtualization security and reduce the risk of data breaches and other security incidents. As virtualization continues to evolve, prioritizing security will be crucial for safeguarding organizational assets and ensuring business continuity.

7.7 Security risks posed by shared images

As virtualization technologies gain traction, the use of shared images—pre-configured templates or snapshots of virtual machines (VMs)—has become commonplace. While shared images streamline deployment and reduce configuration time, they also introduce significant security risks that organizations must address to protect sensitive data and maintain system integrity.

Key Security Risks

- Malware Propagation: Shared images can be infected with malware, either intentionally by malicious actors or inadvertently by users who fail to secure their environments. When organizations deploy a compromised image, they risk propagating malware across multiple VMs, leading to widespread infections and data breaches.

- Vulnerability Inheritance: Shared images often inherit vulnerabilities from the base operating system and applications. If an image contains outdated software or unpatched vulnerabilities, all VMs deployed from that image are at risk. This can result in exploitable weaknesses across multiple systems, making it easier for attackers to compromise the entire environment.

- Sensitive Data Exposure: Pre-configured images may inadvertently contain sensitive information, such as credentials, encryption keys, or proprietary data. If these images are shared without adequate scrutiny, unauthorized users can access sensitive data, leading to potential breaches and compliance violations.

- Misconfiguration Risks: Images may come with default configurations that are not suitable for production environments. If organizations fail to customize security settings post-deployment, they may expose their systems to unnecessary risks, such as weak authentication or excessive permissions.

- Insufficient Access Controls: Shared images often reside in centralized repositories that may not have stringent access controls. If access to these repositories is not properly managed, unauthorized users could download or modify images, leading to potential security incidents.

- Insecure Transfer and Storage: The process of sharing images may involve transferring them across networks, which can expose them to interception. If images are not encrypted during transfer or stored securely, they could be accessed by unauthorized parties.

- Lack of Version Control: Without proper version control, organizations may unknowingly deploy outdated or vulnerable images. This can lead to inconsistencies across environments and make it difficult to track the security posture of deployed VMs.

Mitigating Security Risks

- Regular Image Audits: Organizations should routinely audit shared images to ensure they are free from malware and vulnerabilities. This includes validating installed software, patch levels, and configuration settings.

- Vulnerability Scanning: Implement automated vulnerability scanning tools to assess images for known vulnerabilities before deployment. This proactive approach helps identify and remediate risks before they affect production systems.
- Data Sanitization: Before sharing or deploying images, organizations must ensure that all sensitive data is removed or anonymized. This helps prevent inadvertent exposure of confidential information.
- Access Controls and Permissions: Implement strict access controls for shared image repositories. Ensure that only authorized personnel can upload, download, or modify images, thereby reducing the risk of unauthorized access.
- Use Secure Transfer Methods: Always use secure transfer protocols, such as SFTP or HTTPS, when sharing images to protect against interception. Additionally, consider encrypting images both in transit and at rest.
- Maintain a Version Control System: Implement a version control system for managing shared images. This allows organizations to track changes, roll back to previous versions if needed, and ensure that only the latest, secure images are in use.
- User Training and Awareness: Educate users about the risks associated with shared images and best practices for securing them. This includes emphasizing the importance of validating and customizing images before deployment.

While shared images in virtualization provide significant benefits in terms of efficiency and deployment speed, they also introduce various security risks. By understanding these risks and implementing robust security measures, organizations can mitigate potential vulnerabilities and ensure the integrity of their virtualization environments. Proactive management and continuous monitoring are essential to safeguarding sensitive data and maintaining a secure operating environment.

7.8 Security risks posed by a management OS

A Management Operating System (MOS) is designed to oversee and manage the resources of IT environments, particularly in virtualization and cloud infrastructures. While a MOS is essential for effective resource allocation, monitoring, and orchestration, it also introduces significant security risks that organizations must address to protect sensitive data and maintain operational integrity.

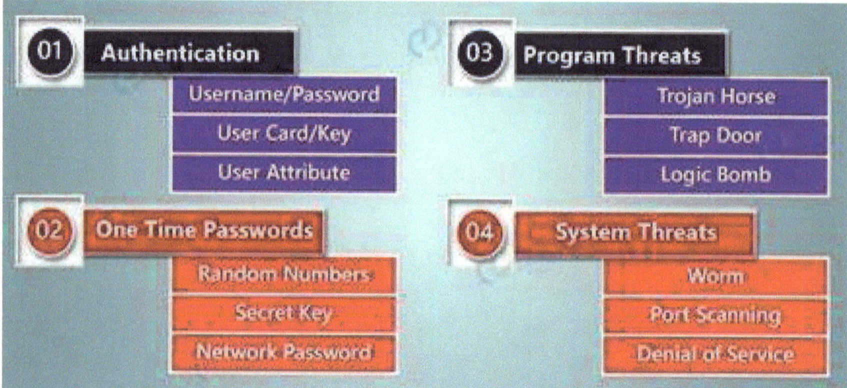

Figure 7.3: Operating System Security

Key Security Risks

- Centralized Vulnerability: The MOS often serves as a central point of control for the entire IT environment. This centralization means that if the MOS is compromised, an attacker can potentially gain access to all managed resources, including sensitive data and critical systems. A single vulnerability in the MOS can lead to widespread exploitation across the entire infrastructure.

- Unauthorized Access: Poor access controls can expose the MOS to unauthorized users. If administrative interfaces are not secured with strong authentication methods, attackers can exploit these weaknesses to gain control of the management layer. Compromised credentials can lead to unauthorized changes, data leaks, or service disruptions.

- Misconfiguration Risks: Management Operating Systems often require complex configurations. Misconfigurations can create security gaps that attackers can exploit. For instance, default settings may not provide adequate security, leaving the system vulnerable to attacks.

- Insecure APIs: Many MOS solutions offer APIs for integration with other tools and systems. If these APIs are not secured properly, they can become entry points for attackers. Weak authentication, lack of encryption, and improper input validation can all expose the MOS to potential attacks.

- Supply Chain Risks: Organizations often rely on third-party tools and plugins to enhance their MOS capabilities. If these third-party solutions have vulnerabilities, they can compromise the security of the entire management system. Attackers may exploit these weaknesses to gain unauthorized access or disrupt services.
- Data Exposure: The MOS typically manages sensitive data, including configuration settings, user credentials, and operational metrics. If this data is not adequately protected—through encryption and access controls—an attacker gaining access to the MOS can easily extract valuable information.
- Denial-of-Service (DoS) Attacks: The MOS is critical for the functionality of the IT environment. A successful DoS attack against the management layer can disrupt operations across the entire infrastructure, leading to downtime and loss of productivity. Attackers may target the MOS to render the environment inoperable.

Mitigating Security Risks

- Strong Authentication and Access Controls: Implement strong, multifactor authentication (MFA) for all administrative access to the MOS. Limit permissions based on the principle of least privilege, ensuring that users only have access to the resources necessary for their roles.
- Regular Security Audits: Conduct regular security assessments and audits of the MOS to identify vulnerabilities and misconfigurations. This includes reviewing access logs, configuration settings, and third-party integrations.
- API Security: Secure APIs by implementing robust authentication mechanisms and encryption. Regularly review and test APIs for vulnerabilities, ensuring that they are not exposed to unauthorized users.
- Data Encryption: Protect sensitive data managed by the MOS with strong encryption, both at rest and in transit. This minimizes the risk of data exposure in the event of a breach.
- Incident Response Plan: Develop a comprehensive incident response plan specifically for the management layer. This plan should outline procedures for detecting, responding to, and recovering from security incidents involving the MOS.

- Vendor Security Assessment: Evaluate the security posture of third-party tools and plugins before integrating them with the MOS. Ensure that they adhere to security best practices and have a track record of addressing vulnerabilities promptly.
- Training and Awareness: Educate staff on the security risks associated with the MOS and best practices for maintaining its security. Continuous training can help mitigate risks stemming from human error.

While a Management Operating System is essential for effective IT resource management, it introduces significant security risks that organizations must proactively address. By implementing robust security measures, conducting regular assessments, and fostering a culture of security awareness, organizations can mitigate these risks and protect their critical infrastructure from potential threats. A strong security posture for the MOS is vital to maintaining the integrity, availability, and confidentiality of the entire IT environment.

7.9 A trusted virtual machine monitor

A Trusted Virtual Machine Monitor (TVMM), also known as a hypervisor, is a specialized layer of software that creates and manages virtual machines (VMs) while ensuring a secure and trusted environment for their operation. As organizations increasingly rely on virtualization for efficiency, scalability, and resource management, the security provided by a TVMM becomes crucial in protecting sensitive data and maintaining system integrity.

Key Features of a Trusted Virtual Machine Monitor

- Isolation: A primary function of a TVMM is to provide strong isolation between VMs. This ensures that if one VM is compromised, the attacker cannot easily access or disrupt other VMs on the same host. Effective isolation prevents data leakage and protects sensitive information across different workloads.
- Integrity Verification: A TVMM should incorporate mechanisms to verify the integrity of both itself and the VMs it manages. Techniques such as cryptographic signatures can be used to ensure that the hypervisor has not been tampered with and that VMs are running trusted code. This is essential for maintaining a secure environment, especially in multi-tenant setups.

- Access Control: Robust access control mechanisms are vital for a TVMM. These controls determine who can create, modify, or manage VMs, helping to prevent unauthorized access and potential breaches. Role-based access controls (RBAC) ensure that only authorized users can perform sensitive operations.
- Secure Boot and Launch: A trusted hypervisor should support secure boot and launch mechanisms, ensuring that only verified and trusted components are loaded during the boot process. This minimizes the risk of boot-level attacks, which can compromise the entire virtualization environment.
- Resource Monitoring and Management: A TVMM must continuously monitor the performance and security of VMs. This includes tracking resource utilization, detecting anomalies, and managing resource allocation to prevent overloading and potential denial-of-service conditions.

Benefits of Using a Trusted Virtual Machine Monitor

- Enhanced Security: By providing a secure and isolated environment for VMs, a TVMM significantly reduces the risk of data breaches and unauthorized access. This is especially important in environments where multiple users or tenants share resources.
- Compliance: Many industries have strict regulatory requirements regarding data protection and privacy. A TVMM that offers robust security features can help organizations comply with regulations such as GDPR, HIPAA, and PCI DSS by ensuring the confidentiality and integrity of sensitive data.
- Improved Trust: A trusted hypervisor fosters trust among users and stakeholders. Organizations can confidently run critical applications and store sensitive data in virtual environments, knowing that the underlying infrastructure is secure.
- Operational Efficiency: With a TVMM, organizations can achieve higher operational efficiency by consolidating workloads and optimizing resource usage. This leads to cost savings and better performance across the IT environment.

Challenges and Considerations
Despite the benefits, deploying a TVMM is not without challenges:

- Complexity: The security of a TVMM is only as strong as its implementation. Poorly configured hypervisors can introduce vulnerabilities. Organizations must ensure that their hypervisors are correctly set up and regularly updated.
- Threat Landscape: As virtualization becomes more widespread, it also becomes a target for attackers. Organizations need to remain vigilant and continuously monitor for emerging threats that could exploit weaknesses in the hypervisor.
- Vendor Dependency: The security of the virtual environment is reliant on the vendor's ability to patch vulnerabilities and provide timely updates. Organizations must choose reputable vendors and stay informed about their security practices.

A Trusted Virtual Machine Monitor plays a vital role in securing virtualization environments, providing strong isolation, integrity verification, and access control. As businesses continue to embrace virtualization, investing in a trusted hypervisor is essential for protecting sensitive data, ensuring compliance, and maintaining operational efficiency. By leveraging the security features of a TVMM, organizations can navigate the complexities of modern IT infrastructures with confidence.

CHAPTER EIGHT

Advanced Topics in Cloud Computing

8.1 Energy efficiency in clouds

Energy efficiency in cloud computing is a critical aspect of modern IT infrastructure, driven by the need for sustainability and cost-effectiveness. As businesses increasingly rely on cloud services, the demand for data centers continues to rise, leading to higher energy consumption. Thus, improving energy efficiency in cloud environments is essential for reducing both operational costs and environmental impact.

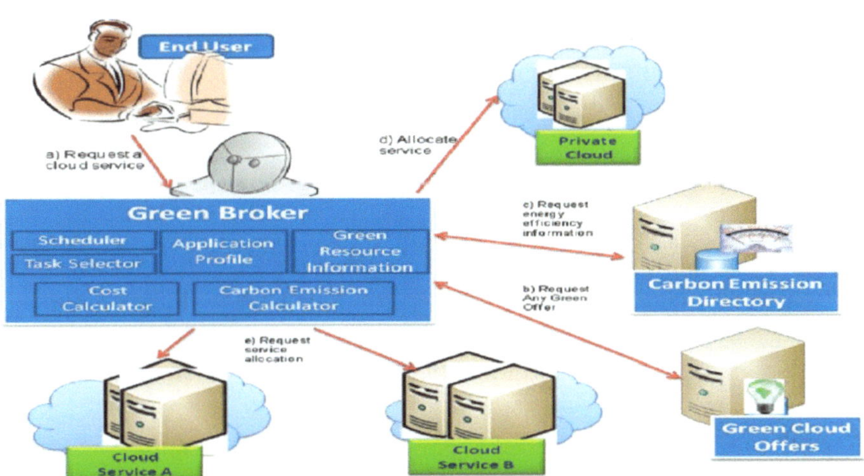

Figure 8.1: Energy Efficiency in Cloud Computing

The Importance of Energy Efficiency

Data centers are among the most energy-intensive facilities, with significant amounts of electricity consumed for powering servers, cooling systems, and supporting infrastructure. Energy efficiency in the cloud not only helps to lower electricity bills but also minimizes the carbon footprint associated with extensive computing activities. As organizations strive to meet regulatory requirements and corporate sustainability goals, energy-efficient cloud solutions are becoming a key competitive differentiator.

Strategies for Improving Energy Efficiency

- Virtualization: Virtualization technology allows multiple virtual machines (VMs) to run on a single physical server. This maximizes resource utilization and reduces the number of physical servers needed, thereby lowering energy consumption for both computing and cooling.
- Server Optimization: Advanced hardware design and energy-efficient components, such as low-power processors and SSDs, contribute to reducing energy use. Cloud providers are increasingly adopting energy-efficient servers that provide better performance per watt.
- Dynamic Resource Allocation: Using orchestration tools and automated scaling can optimize resource allocation based on real-time demand. This means that resources are only utilized when needed, reducing idle times and conserving energy.
- Efficient Cooling Systems: Traditional cooling methods can be inefficient. Innovative cooling solutions, such as liquid cooling or outside air economization, can significantly reduce energy use. Data centers are also employing techniques like hot and cold aisle containment to improve airflow efficiency.
- Renewable Energy Sources: Many cloud providers are investing in renewable energy sources to power their data centers. By sourcing energy from solar, wind, or hydroelectric systems, they can lower the carbon footprint of their operations and appeal to environmentally conscious clients.
- Energy Management Software: Advanced software solutions monitor energy usage in real-time, providing insights into consumption patterns. This data can be used to optimize operations, schedule maintenance during off-peak hours, and identify areas for improvement.

Measuring Energy Efficiency

Energy efficiency can be quantified using metrics like Power Usage Effectiveness (PUE), which measures the ratio of total building energy usage to the energy used by the IT equipment alone. A lower PUE indicates better energy efficiency. Other metrics include Carbon Usage Effectiveness (CUE) and Data Center Infrastructure Efficiency (DCIE), which help organizations benchmark and track improvements over time.

Challenges and Future Directions

Despite the advancements in energy efficiency, challenges remain. The rapid growth of cloud computing can lead to increased energy demand, and maintaining a balance between performance and efficiency is critical. Moreover, as AI and machine learning applications become more prevalent, they require substantial computational resources, potentially offsetting efficiency gains.

To address these challenges, ongoing research and development in energy-efficient technologies and practices are essential. Collaboration between cloud providers, technology manufacturers, and regulatory bodies can drive innovation and set industry standards that promote sustainable practices.

8.2 Market-based management of clouds

Market-based management of cloud computing represents an innovative approach to resource allocation, pricing, and service delivery in cloud environments. By leveraging market principles, cloud providers can optimize efficiency, enhance competitiveness, and better meet the dynamic needs of customers.

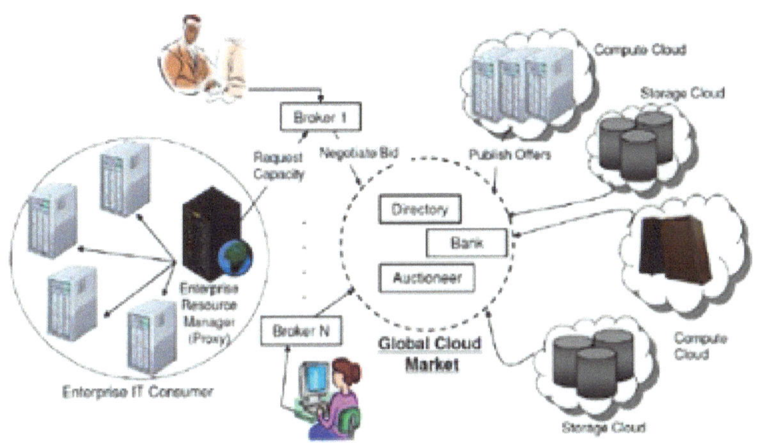

Figure 8.2 Market based management of cloud

The Concept of Market-Based Management

Market-based management involves applying economic principles to the operation and governance of cloud services. This approach allows for flexible resource allocation, enabling users to bid for resources based on their requirements. It fosters competition among service providers, leading to better pricing and quality of service.

Key Features

- Dynamic Pricing Models: Cloud providers can implement dynamic pricing strategies based on supply and demand. For example, during peak usage times, prices can rise, encouraging users to shift workloads to off-peak periods. This not only helps manage demand but also maximizes revenue for providers.
- Resource Auctions: In a market-based model, resources can be auctioned to customers. Users can place bids for computing power or storage, and resources are allocated to the highest bidders. This competitive bidding can lead to more efficient utilization of resources, ensuring that they are directed to those who value them most.
- Service Level Agreements (SLAs) as Contracts: SLAs can be treated as contractual agreements that specify performance metrics, availability, and penalties for non-compliance. This approach encourages cloud providers to meet their commitments and gives customers the ability to choose providers based on service quality and reliability.
- Consumer Choice and Transparency: Market-based management emphasizes transparency in pricing and service options. Customers can compare services across multiple providers, leading to informed decisions. This competition drives providers to improve their offerings and innovate continuously.

Benefits

- Enhanced Efficiency: By allowing users to bid for resources, cloud providers can optimize resource allocation, reducing waste and improving overall efficiency. Resources are dynamically adjusted to meet demand, leading to better utilization.

- Cost Savings: Dynamic pricing and competitive bidding can lower costs for consumers. Organizations can take advantage of lower prices during off-peak times, significantly reducing their cloud spending.
- Incentivized Innovation: The competitive nature of market-based management encourages cloud providers to innovate continuously. Providers must enhance their services and reduce costs to attract and retain customers, fostering a culture of improvement.
- Tailored Services: Customers can choose from a variety of services and pricing models, enabling them to select options that best fit their needs. This flexibility can lead to increased satisfaction and loyalty.

Challenges

Despite its advantages, market-based management also presents challenges:

- Complexity: Implementing a market-based system requires sophisticated algorithms and management tools. Ensuring a seamless experience for users can be complex, especially in balancing supply and demand.
- Market Volatility: Price fluctuations can lead to unpredictability in budgeting for organizations. Businesses need to develop strategies to manage costs in a dynamic pricing environment.
- Quality Assurance: As providers compete on price, there may be a risk of compromising service quality. It is crucial for providers to maintain high standards while remaining competitive.

Future Directions

The future of market-based management in clouds will likely involve advancements in artificial intelligence and machine learning to predict demand and optimize pricing dynamically. Additionally, the integration of blockchain technology could enhance transparency and trust in transactions, further strengthening market mechanisms.

8.3 Federated clouds/InterCloud

Federated clouds, often referred to as the InterCloud, represent a paradigm shift in cloud computing, enabling multiple cloud service providers to interconnect and collaborate seamlessly. This approach enhances resource availability, scalability, and service diversity, ultimately benefiting users with a more robust and flexible computing environment.

Concept of Federated Clouds

Federated clouds are formed by linking various independent cloud infrastructures, allowing them to function as a unified system. Each cloud retains its autonomy while sharing resources, services, and data with other clouds in the federation. This interconnectivity addresses challenges such as resource limitations, vendor lock-in, and varying service levels.

Key Features

- Interoperability: A critical aspect of federated clouds is the ability to achieve interoperability among different cloud environments. This requires standardization of protocols and APIs, allowing seamless data exchange and service integration across diverse platforms.
- Resource Sharing: Federated clouds enable organizations to share resources dynamically. If one cloud experiences high demand, it can access additional resources from another cloud within the federation, ensuring that applications remain responsive and reliable.
- Service Diversification: Users can choose from a broader array of services offered by different providers within the federation. This diversification allows businesses to tailor their cloud solutions to specific needs, leveraging the best capabilities from multiple vendors.
- Data Sovereignty: Federated clouds can address data sovereignty concerns by allowing organizations to keep their data within specific geographical boundaries while still benefiting from the global resources of the federation.
- Benefits
- Enhanced Scalability: By connecting multiple clouds, federated systems can easily scale resources up or down based on demand. This elasticity ensures that businesses can adapt to changing workloads without significant investment in infrastructure.
- Improved Resilience and Reliability: Federated clouds provide redundancy and failover options. If one cloud provider experiences downtime, users can seamlessly transition to another cloud, ensuring business continuity.
- Cost Efficiency: Organizations can optimize their spending by using the most cost-effective resources from various clouds. This flexibility helps minimize operational costs while maximizing performance.
- Vendor Independence: Federated clouds mitigate the risk of vendor lock-in by allowing organizations to diversify their cloud usage. Businesses can shift workloads among different providers, maintaining control over

their cloud strategy.

Challenges
While the concept of federated clouds offers significant advantages, it also presents challenges:

- Complex Management: Managing multiple cloud environments can be complex. Organizations need robust orchestration and management tools to oversee resource allocation, performance monitoring, and security across federated clouds.
- Security and Compliance: Data security becomes more challenging in a federated environment, as data moves between different clouds. Organizations must ensure that all providers meet stringent security and compliance standards.
- Interoperability Issues: Achieving true interoperability requires standardization, which can be difficult in a landscape where many cloud providers have proprietary technologies. Developing common protocols is essential for the success of federated clouds.

Future Directions
The future of federated clouds is likely to be shaped by advancements in technologies such as artificial intelligence, machine learning, and blockchain. AI can enhance resource management and optimization, while blockchain can improve security and transparency in transactions. Additionally, as organizations continue to prioritize data privacy and sovereignty, federated cloud solutions will evolve to address these needs effectively.

8.4 Third-party cloud services
Third-party cloud services have become integral to modern business operations, offering a wide array of resources and solutions that enhance flexibility, scalability, and cost-effectiveness. These services, provided by external vendors, allow organizations to leverage advanced technologies without the burden of maintaining their own infrastructure.

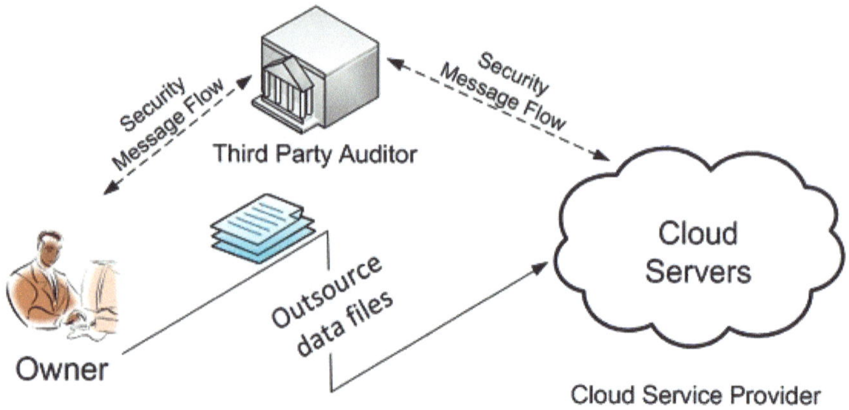

Figure: 8.3 Third-party cloud services

Overview of Third-Party Cloud Services

Third-party cloud services encompass a variety of offerings, including Infrastructure as a Service (IaaS), Platform as a Service (PaaS), and Software as a Service (SaaS). Each of these models serves different business needs:

- Infrastructure as a Service (IaaS): This model provides virtualized computing resources over the internet. Organizations can rent servers, storage, and networking capabilities on a pay-as-you-go basis. Popular examples include Amazon Web Services (AWS) and Microsoft Azure, which allow businesses to scale infrastructure according to demand.
- Platform as a Service (PaaS): PaaS offers a platform that enables developers to build, test, and deploy applications without managing the underlying infrastructure. This model streamlines the development process, allowing for quicker deployment and updates. Examples include Google App Engine and Heroku.
- Software as a Service (SaaS): SaaS delivers software applications over the internet, accessible via a web browser. This eliminates the need for installation and maintenance on local devices. Notable SaaS products include Salesforce, Google Workspace, and Slack, which provide various tools for productivity, collaboration, and customer relationship management.

Benefits of Third-Party Cloud Services

- Cost Efficiency: Utilizing third-party cloud services can significantly reduce capital expenditures. Organizations avoid the costs associated with purchasing and maintaining hardware, as they pay only for the resources they use.
- Scalability and Flexibility: Third-party services offer the ability to scale resources up or down based on demand. Businesses can quickly adjust their cloud resources to accommodate growth, seasonal fluctuations, or unexpected spikes in activity.
- Access to Advanced Technologies: Third-party cloud providers often invest in cutting-edge technology and security measures. Organizations can benefit from these advancements without the need to develop them in-house.
- Focus on Core Business: By outsourcing cloud infrastructure and services, businesses can concentrate on their core competencies rather than managing IT resources. This strategic focus can drive innovation and enhance competitiveness.

Challenges

Despite the many advantages, relying on third-party cloud services also poses several challenges:

- Vendor Lock-In: Organizations may become dependent on a single provider's ecosystem, making it difficult to switch to another service without incurring significant costs or operational disruptions.
- Data Security and Compliance: Entrusting sensitive data to third-party providers raises concerns about security and regulatory compliance. Businesses must ensure that their providers adhere to strict security standards and data protection regulations.
- Service Reliability: While many cloud providers offer robust SLAs (Service Level Agreements), outages and downtime can still occur. Organizations must evaluate the reliability and performance track records of their chosen providers.
- Limited Customization: Third-party solutions may not always fit specific business needs. Customization options can be limited compared to in-house solutions, potentially leading to inefficiencies.

Future Trends

The landscape of third-party cloud services is continually evolving. Emerging trends include:

- Hybrid and Multi-Cloud Strategies: Many organizations are adopting hybrid and multi-cloud approaches to leverage the strengths of various providers while mitigating risks associated with vendor lock-in.
- Increased Focus on Security: As cyber threats become more sophisticated, third-party providers are enhancing their security measures and compliance frameworks to meet customer expectations.
- AI and Automation Integration: Cloud services are increasingly integrating artificial intelligence and automation tools, enabling organizations to streamline processes and improve decision-making.

CHAPTER NINE

Practical Approches

Practical -1 Study of Public Cloud : Amazon Web Services EC2, Google AppEngine, Microsoft Azure

Solustion:

Studying public cloud services like Amazon Web Services (AWS) EC2, Google App Engine, and Microsoft Azure involves understanding their features, strengths, and use cases. Here's a breakdown of each service:

Amazon Web Services (AWS) EC2

Overview:

- AWS Elastic Compute Cloud (EC2) provides scalable computing capacity in the cloud, allowing users to run virtual servers.

Key Features:

- Scalability: Easily scale up or down based on demand.
- Diverse Instance Types: Offers a variety of instance types optimized for different tasks (compute, memory, storage).
- Pay-as-You-Go Pricing: Only pay for what you use, which can be cost-effective for variable workloads.
- Security: Comprehensive security features, including Virtual Private Cloud (VPC) and IAM (Identity and Access Management).
- Global Reach: Multiple availability zones and regions to enhance redundancy and disaster recovery.

Use Cases:

- Hosting applications, batch processing, big data analytics, and web hosting.

Google App Engine

Overview:

Google App Engine is a Platform as a Service (PaaS) that allows developers to build and host applications without managing the underlying infrastructure.

Key Features:

- Managed Environment: Automatic scaling, load balancing, and health monitoring.
- Support for Multiple Languages: Supports several programming languages, including Python, Java, Go, and PHP.
- Integrated Services: Seamless integration with Google Cloud services, such as BigQuery and Firebase.
- Versioning: Allows deployment of multiple versions of an app simultaneously.

Use Cases:

- Web applications, mobile backends, and APIs, particularly for applications requiring rapid development and scaling.

Microsoft Azure

Overview:

- Microsoft Azure offers a comprehensive suite of cloud services, including Infrastructure as a Service (IaaS) and PaaS, catering to a wide range of applications.

Key Features:

- Hybrid Cloud Capabilities: Strong support for hybrid cloud scenarios, allowing integration with on-premises data centers.
- Extensive Services Portfolio: Wide range of services including AI, machine learning, IoT, and databases.
- Enterprise Integration: Seamless integration with Microsoft products (e.g., Office 365, Dynamics 365).
- Robust Security and Compliance: Advanced security features and compliance certifications.

Use Cases:

- Enterprise applications, data analytics, IoT solutions, and development environments.

Comparison
Deployment Models:

- AWS EC2 focuses on providing raw compute power and flexibility.
- Google App Engine abstracts infrastructure management, focusing on app development.
- Azure offers a mix of IaaS and PaaS, with strong hybrid capabilities.

Pricing Models:
AWS follows a pay-as-you-go model.

- Google App Engine provides a flexible pricing model based on usage.
- Azure has various pricing options, including pay-as-you-go and reserved instances.

Target Users:

- AWS EC2 is suited for businesses needing granular control over their compute resources.
- Google App Engine is ideal for developers looking for ease of use and rapid deployment.
- Azure targets enterprises, especially those already using Microsoft technologies.

Conclusion

Choosing the right public cloud service depends on specific needs, such as scalability, ease of management, integration requirements, and existing technology stacks. Understanding the strengths and weaknesses of AWS EC2, Google App Engine, and Microsoft Azure will help in making informed decisions tailored to your organization's goals.

Practical -2 Study of Open Source Cloud Technology : CloudSim, Aneka, Eucalyptus Google Drive, Google Docs and Google Slides must be used for hosting e-books, important articles and presentations

respectively.

Solustion:

Studying open-source cloud technologies involves exploring platforms that facilitate cloud computing and resource management. Here's a detailed look at CloudSim, Aneka, and Eucalyptus, along with how Google Drive, Google Docs, and Google Slides can be utilized for hosting e-books, important articles, and presentations.

Open Source Cloud Technologies

1. CloudSim

Overview:

- CloudSim is a simulation framework that allows researchers and developers to model and simulate cloud computing environments.

Key Features:

- Resource Management: Simulates various cloud infrastructure components, including data centers, virtual machines, and applications.
- Extensibility: Users can extend the framework to model different cloud scenarios and algorithms.
- Evaluation: Facilitates performance evaluation of cloud services, which is useful for research and development.

Use Cases:

- Academic research, cloud resource management studies, and algorithm testing in cloud environments.

2. Aneka

Overview:

- Aneka is a cloud computing platform that provides a framework for deploying and managing applications in the cloud.

Key Features:

- Multi-Cloud Support: Can deploy applications across multiple cloud environments.

- Resource Management: Allows for dynamic resource allocation and scheduling of tasks.
- Programming Model: Supports various programming models, including MapReduce and Batch processing.

Use Cases:

- Enterprise application deployment, distributed computing, and workload management.

3. Eucalyptus
Overview:

- Eucalyptus is an open-source software platform for building private clouds, enabling users to create their own cloud environments.

Key Features:

- AWS Compatibility: Provides an API compatible with Amazon Web Services, making it easier to migrate applications between public and private clouds.
- Scalability: Supports the scaling of resources based on demand.
- Hybrid Cloud Capabilities: Allows for seamless integration with public cloud resources.

Use Cases:

- Organizations looking to create private clouds while leveraging existing infrastructure.
- Hosting Documents with Google Services

Google Drive
Use Case:
E-Books and Important Articles:

- Google Drive can be used to store and share e-books and important articles in various formats (PDF, Word, etc.). Its collaborative features allow multiple users to access, comment on, and edit documents.

Key Features:

- Storage: Offers substantial free and paid storage options.
- Sharing and Collaboration: Easily share documents with specific people or groups.
- Accessibility: Accessible from any device with internet access.

Google Docs
Use Case:
Hosting Important Articles:

- Google Docs is ideal for writing, editing, and hosting important articles. Multiple users can collaborate in real-time, making it easy to draft and revise content together.

Key Features:

- Real-Time Collaboration: Allows simultaneous editing by multiple users.
- Version History: Tracks changes and allows users to revert to previous versions.
- Integration: Easily integrates with Google Drive for storage.

Google Slides
Use Case:
Presentations:

- Google Slides is perfect for creating and hosting presentations. It allows for collaboration and sharing, making it easy for teams to work on presentations together.

Key Features:

- Presentation Tools: Offers a variety of templates and design options.
- Collaboration: Similar to Docs, allows multiple users to edit and comment in real-time.
- Sharing: Presentations can be easily shared via links or directly through Google Drive.

Conclusion

Open-source cloud technologies like CloudSim, Aneka, and Eucalyptus provide valuable tools for simulating, managing, and deploying cloud resources. Meanwhile, Google Drive, Docs, and Slides offer effective solutions for hosting and collaborating on e-books, articles, and presentations. Each of these tools has distinct advantages depending on the specific needs of users and organizations, making them suitable for various cloud computing and collaboration scenarios.

Practical -3 Practical Approach for understanding virtualization concept using VmWare Workstation.

Solustion:

Understanding virtualization concepts through VMware Workstation can be an effective hands-on approach. Here's a practical guide to get you started:

Overview of Virtualization

Virtualization allows multiple operating systems to run on a single physical machine by creating virtual environments. VMware Workstation is a powerful desktop virtualization software that enables users to create and manage virtual machines (VMs).

Step-by-Step Guide

1. Installation of VMware Workstation

Download and Install:

- Visit the VMware website and download the latest version of VMware Workstation (Playcr or Pro).
- Follow the installation instructions specific to your operating system.

2. Creating Your First Virtual Machine

Open VMware Workstation:

- Launch the application after installation.

Create a New VM:

- Click on "Create a New Virtual Machine."
- Choose the configuration type: "Typical" is recommended for beginners.

Select Installation Media:

Choose to install the OS from a physical disk, ISO image, or other media. For practice, downloading an ISO of a Linux distribution (like Ubuntu) is recommended.

Configure VM Settings:

- Name the VM: Give your virtual machine a name.
- Location: Specify where you want to save the VM files.
- Select OS Type: Choose the operating system type (e.g., Linux, Windows).

Allocate Resources:

- CPU: Assign the number of processors/cores.
- Memory: Set the amount of RAM for the VM.
- Disk Space: Create a virtual hard disk with appropriate size (e.g., 20GB).

3. Understanding Virtual Hardware Configuration
Edit VM Settings:

- After creating the VM, right-click on it and select "Settings."
- Explore virtual hardware settings, including:
- Processors: Adjust the number of virtual CPUs.
- Memory: Change allocated RAM.
- Network Adapter: Configure how the VM connects to the internet (NAT, Bridged, Host-Only).
- USB Controller: Manage USB device support.

4. Installing the Operating System
Start the VM:

- Click on "Power on this virtual machine."
- Follow the prompts to install the operating system from the selected media.
- Complete OS Installation:
- Configure the OS as you would on a physical machine (create user accounts, settings, etc.).

5. Exploring Virtualization Concepts

Snapshots:

- Take a snapshot of the VM after installation. This allows you to revert to this state later.
- Experiment with the VM (install software, change settings) and take additional snapshots.

Cloning:

- Create clones of your VM. This allows you to have multiple instances with the same configuration.

Virtual Networks:

- Experiment with different network settings (NAT vs. Bridged) and observe the differences in connectivity.

Resource Allocation:

- Adjust CPU and memory allocation while the VM is running to see how it affects performance.

6. Using VMware Tools

Install VMware Tools:

After installing the OS, install VMware Tools within the VM. This enhances performance and adds features like improved graphics and shared clipboard.

7. Advanced Features

Shared Folders:

- Set up shared folders between the host and the VM for easy file transfer.

Multiple VMs:

- Create additional VMs and connect them in a virtual network. Test communication between them.

Performance Monitoring:

- Use the built-in monitoring tools to observe resource usage and performance metrics.

Conclusion

Using VMware Workstation to explore virtualization concepts provides practical experience with creating, managing, and understanding virtual machines. By following this hands-on approach, you'll gain insights into the key principles of virtualization, including resource allocation, networking, and system management. This knowledge can be valuable for various applications, including development, testing, and IT infrastructure management.

Practical -4 Study how to create a Collaborative learning environment for a particular learning topic using Google Apps. Google Drive, Google Docs and Google Slides must be used for hosting e-books, important articles and presentations respectively.

Solustion:

Creating a collaborative learning environment using Google Apps involves leveraging Google Drive, Docs, and Slides effectively.

- **Google Drive:** Start by creating a shared folder for the specific learning topic. This central repository will host e-books and important articles, making resources easily accessible to all participants. Ensure appropriate sharing settings for collaborative access.
- **Google Docs:** Use Docs for collaborative writing and note-taking. Participants can co-create study guides, summarize articles, or draft reflections, allowing for real-time feedback and discussion. Incorporate comments and suggestions to foster dialogue.
- **Google Slides:** Utilize Slides for presentations on the topic. Each group member can contribute slides, promoting teamwork and diverse perspectives. This can culminate in a virtual presentation session where participants share their insights.

By integrating these tools, learners can engage actively, share resources, and build knowledge collectively, enhancing the overall learning experience.

Practical -5 Modeling and simulation Cloud computing environments, including Data Centers, Hosts and Cloudlets and perform VM provisioning using CloudSim Design a host with two CPU cores, which

receives request for hosting two VMs, such that each one requires two cores and plans to host four tasks units. More specifically, tasks t1, t2, t3 and t4 to be hosted in VM1, while t5, t6, t7, and t8 to be hosted in VM2. Implement space-shared allocation policy. Compare the results.

Solustion:

To model and simulate a cloud computing environment using CloudSim, we can design a host with specific configurations and implement a space-shared allocation policy for the virtual machines (VMs). Below is a structured approach to setting this up:

Environment Setup

CloudSim Configuration:

- Ensure you have the CloudSim library integrated into your Java project.

Create the Host:

- The host will have two CPU cores, and it will be responsible for hosting two VMs.
- Each VM will require two CPU cores.

Implementation Steps

Define the Host:

```
// Creating a host with two CPU cores
List<Pe> cpuList = new ArrayList<>();
int mips - 1000; // MIPS per core
for (int i = 0; i < 2; i++) {
cpuList.add(new Pe(i, new PeProvisionerSimple(mips)));
}
Host host = new Host(0, new RamProvisionerSimple(2048), new BwProvisionerSimple(10000),
10000, cpuList, new VmSchedulerSpaceShared(cpuList));
```

Create the Virtual Machines:

- **Each VM requires two CPU cores.**

```
// VM1 with two cores
Vm vm1 = new Vm(0, 0, 1000, 2, 512, 1000, new CloudletSchedulerSpaceShared());
```

```
// VM2 with two cores
Vm vm2 = new Vm(1, 0, 1000, 2, 512, 1000, new
CloudletSchedulerSpaceShared());
```

Create Cloudlets:

- **Define tasks t1, t2, t3, t4 for VM1 and t5, t6, t7, t8 for VM2.**

```
List<Cloudlet> cloudletList = new ArrayList<>();
for (int i = 1; i <= 8; i++) {
Cloudlet cloudlet = new Cloudlet(i, 4000, 1, 300, 300, new
UtilizationModelStochastic());
if (i <= 4) {
cloudlet.setVmId(vm1.getId());
} else {
cloudlet.setVmId(vm2.getId());
}
cloudletList.add(cloudlet);
}
```

Simulate the Environment:

- **Add VMs to the host and execute the simulation.**

```
Datacenter datacenter = new Datacenter("Datacenter", new
DatacenterCharacteristics(...), new VmAllocationPolicySimple(hostList),
new ArrayList<>(), 0);
datacenter.getHostList().get(0).addVm(vm1);
datacenter.getHostList().get(0).addVm(vm2);
// Start the simulation
CloudSim.startSimulation();
```

Collect and Compare Results:

- **After simulation, retrieve and compare the metrics (execution time, waiting time, etc.) for the tasks in both VMs.**

```
List<Cloudlet> finishedCloudlets = broker.getCloudletReceivedList();
for (Cloudlet cloudlet : finishedCloudlets) {
System.out.println("Cloudlet ID: " + cloudlet.getId() + " Status: " +
cloudlet.getStatus() + " Execution Time: " + cloudlet.getActualCPUTime());
```

```
}
```

Comparison of Results

- Execution Time: Compare the actual execution times of tasks in VM1 and VM2. Given the space-shared policy, tasks will execute concurrently but share resources.
- Resource Utilization: Analyze the CPU utilization per VM and overall host efficiency.
- Wait Times: Review the queue lengths and waiting times for each task to understand the impact of space-sharing.

Conclusion

By simulating the environment as described, you can observe how the space-shared allocation policy affects task execution across two VMs on a dual-core host. The comparison of results will provide insights into resource allocation efficiency and performance under the given constraints.

Practical -6 Modeling and simulation Cloud computing environments, including Data Centers, Hosts and Cloudlets and perform VM provisioning using CloudSim Design a host with two CPU cores, which receives request for hosting two VMs, such that each one requires two cores and plans to host four tasks units. More specifically, tasks t1, t2, t3 and t4 to be hosted in VM1, while t5, t6, t7, and t8 to be hosted in VM2. Implement time-share allocation policy. Compare the results.

Solustion:

To model a cloud computing environment using CloudSim, you can follow these steps to design a host with two CPU cores, provision two VMs, and implement a time-share allocation policy:

Step 1: Set Up CloudSim Environment

Initialize CloudSim:

```
CloudSim.init(1, Calendar.getInstance(), false);
```

Create Data Center:

```
DatacenterCharacteristics characteristics = new DatacenterCharacteristics(
"x86", "Linux", "Xen", 1.0,
new HashMap<>(), new ArrayList<>(), 0, 0);
Datacenter datacenter = new Datacenter("Datacenter", characteristics, new VmAllocationPolicySimple(), new ArrayList<>(), 0);
```

Step 2: Create Host

Configure Host

```
List<Pe> peList = new ArrayList<>();
peList.add(new Pe(0, new PeProvisionerSimple(1000))); // Core 1
peList.add(new Pe(1, new PeProvisionerSimple(1000))); // Core 2
Host host = new Host(0, new RamProvisionerSimple(2048),
new        BwProvisionerSimple(10000),        10000,        peList,        new
ArrayList<Storage>());
```

Step 3: Create Virtual Machines

Create VMs:

```
Vm      vm1      =      new      Vm(0,    1,    1000,    2,    1000,    new
CloudletSchedulerTimeShared());
Vm      vm2      =      new      Vm(1,    1,    1000,    2,    1000,    new
CloudletSchedulerTimeShared());
```

Step 4: Create Cloudlets (Tasks)

Create Cloudlets:

```
List<Cloudlet> cloudletList = new ArrayList<>();
for (int i = 0; i < 4; i++) {
cloudletList.add(new      Cloudlet(i,      4000,      1,      300,      300,      new
UtilizationModelStochastic()));
}
for (int i = 4; i < 8; i++) {
cloudletList.add(new      Cloudlet(i,      4000,      1,      300,      300,      new
UtilizationModelStochastic()));
}
```

Step 5: Assign Cloudlets to VMs

Assign Tasks:

```
for (int i = 0; i < 4; i++) {
cloudletList.get(i).setVmId(vm1.getId());
}
for (int i = 4; i < 8; i++) {
cloudletList.get(i).setVmId(vm2.getId());
}
```

Step 6: Start Simulation

Start Simulation:

```
datacenter.getHostList().get(0).addVm(vm1);
datacenter.getHostList().get(0).addVm(vm2);
CloudSim.startSimulation();
```

Step 7: Collect and Compare Results

Get Results:

```
List<Cloudlet> processedCloudlets = cloudletList;
for (Cloudlet cloudlet : processedCloudlets) {
System.out.println("Cloudlet  ID:  "  +  cloudlet.getId()  +  "  Status:  "  +
cloudlet.getStatus());
// Display additional metrics if needed
}
```

Step 8: Analyze Performance

- After running the simulation, compare the performance metrics of VM1 and VM2, such as:
- Completion Time: Analyze how long each VM took to finish its tasks.
- CPU Utilization: Measure the CPU usage for both VMs.
- Response Time: Evaluate how quickly tasks were processed.

Conclusion

This model demonstrates a simple cloud environment with two VMs sharing resources through a time-sharing allocation policy. By comparing the metrics, you can gain insights into resource allocation efficiency and VM performance in a cloud computing context.

Practical -7 Create and launch a virtual machine instance on Eucalyptus cloud and access that virtual machine using putty client.

Solustion:

Creating and launching a virtual machine instance on Eucalyptus Cloud and accessing it with PuTTY involves several steps. Here's a step-by-step guide:

Step 1: Set Up Eucalyptus Environment

- Install Eucalyptus: Ensure that Eucalyptus is properly installed and configured on your cloud infrastructure. You'll need admin access to create and manage instances.
- Configure User Access: Ensure you have a user account set up with the necessary permissions to launch instances.

Step 2: Create a Key Pair

- Access Eucalyptus Management Console: Open the Eucalyptus management console (usually at a URL like http://<your-eucalyptus-

url>:<port>).
- Create Key Pair:
- Navigate to the "Key Pairs" section.
- Click "Create Key Pair."
- Download the private key file (usually in .pem format). Save it securely.

Step 3: Launch a Virtual Machine Instance
Select the Instance Type:

- Go to the "Instances" section in the management console.
- Click on "Launch Instance."
- Choose an Amazon Machine Image (AMI) from the list.

Configure Instance:

- Select the instance type (e.g., t2.micro).
- Configure other settings like network, storage, and security groups.
- Make sure to add your key pair from Step 2.

Launch the Instance:

- Review your settings and click "Launch."
- Step 4: Obtain the Instance's Public IP Address

Check Instance Status:

- Once the instance is launched, it will take a few moments to become active. Check the status in the "Instances" section.

Find Public IP:

- Once running, note the public IP address assigned to your instance.

Step 5: Access the Instance with PuTTY
Convert .pem to .ppk:

- PuTTY uses .ppk files for SSH keys. Use PuTTYgen (comes with PuTTY) to convert your .pem key.

- Open PuTTYgen, click "Load," and select your .pem file.
- Click "Save private key" to save the key in .ppk format.

Open PuTTY:

- In the PuTTY configuration window, enter the public IP address of your instance in the "Host Name (or IP address)" field.

Configure SSH Key:

- In the left panel, navigate to Connection > SSH > Auth.
- Browse for your converted .ppk file.

Connect to the Instance:

- Click "Open" to start the SSH session.
- If prompted, enter the username for your AMI (common ones are ubuntu, ec2-user, or root).

Step 6: Finalize Connection

- Once connected, you should have access to the terminal of your Eucalyptus instance.
- You can now start configuring your VM or deploy applications as needed.

Troubleshooting

- Connection Issues: Ensure that your security group settings allow SSH (port 22) from your IP address.
- Instance Status: Make sure your instance is running and that you are using the correct public IP address.

Following these steps should enable you to successfully create, launch, and access a virtual machine instance on Eucalyptus Cloud using the PuTTY client.

Practical -8 Implement Private cloud Infrastructure (Cloud-in-a-Box) using Eucalyptus.

Solustion:

Setting up a private cloud infrastructure using Eucalyptus (often referred to as "Cloud-in-a-Box") involves several steps, including installation, configuration, and management. Below is a comprehensive guide to help you set up Eucalyptus for a private cloud.

Step 1: Prepare Your Environment

System Requirements:

- Ensure you have a dedicated server or virtual machine with a supported OS (usually Ubuntu or CentOS).
- Recommended hardware: 8 GB RAM, 4 CPU cores, and sufficient disk space (at least 20 GB).

Install Dependencies:

- Update your system and install required packages:

```
sudo apt update && sudo apt upgrade -y
sudo apt install -y wget curl python3 python3-pip
```

Step 2: Install Eucalyptus

Add Eucalyptus Repository:

- For Ubuntu:

```
echo "deb http://downloads.eucalyptus.com/software/eucalyptus/4.5/
ubuntu focal main" | sudo tee /etc/apt/sources.list.d/eucalyptus.list
wget -qO - http://downloads.eucalyptus.com/software/eucalyptus/4.5/
ubuntu/KEY.gpg | sudo apt-key add -
sudo apt update
```

Install Eucalyptus:

- Install the Eucalyptus components

```
sudo apt install eucalyptus
```

Step 3: Configure Eucalyptus

Set Up Eucalyptus:

- Run the configuration script:

```
sudo /usr/sbin/euca-conf --setup
```

- Follow the prompts to configure the cloud settings.

Configure Networking:

- Ensure that the necessary ports are open (especially for EC2 API, Walrus, and the storage service).

Configure the Cloud Controller (CC):

- The CC is responsible for managing the cloud. Edit the configuration file:

```
sudo nano /etc/eucalyptus/eucalyptus.conf
```

- Configure network settings, security groups, and storage configurations as per your requirements.

Step 4: Set Up Node Controllers (NC)
Install Node Controller:

- On each compute node that will run VMs:

```
sudo apt install eucalyptus-nc
```
Configure Node Controller:

- Edit the NC configuration file:

```
sudo nano /etc/eucalyptus/eucalyptus.conf
```

- Ensure it points to the correct CC and configure networking.

Start the Node Controller:
```
sudo systemctl start eucalyptus-nc
```
Step 5: Start Services
Start the Cloud Controller:
```
sudo systemctl start eucalyptus-cc
```
Verify Services:

- Check that all services are running:

sudo systemctl status eucalyptus-cc eucalyptus-nc
Step 6: Access the Eucalyptus Management Console
Access the Console:

- Open a web browser and go to http://<your-server-ip>:<port> (default port is 8080).
- Log in with the credentials created during the setup.

Step 7: Create a Key Pair
Create a Key Pair:

- In the management console, navigate to the Key Pairs section and create a new key pair. Download the private key file (.pem).

Step 8: Launch Instances
Launch an Instance:

- Select an AMI from the list available.
- Choose instance type and configure security groups.
- Launch the instance.

Step 9: Access Instances
Connect Using SSH:

- Use an SSH client (like PuTTY) to access your instance using the private key created earlier.

Step 10: Monitoring and Management
Monitor Your Cloud:

- Use the management console to monitor instances, usage statistics, and resource allocation.

Scaling and Management:

- Adjust the number of node controllers and other configurations as your needs grow.

Troubleshooting Tips

- Service Issues: Check logs in /var/log/eucalyptus/ for error messages.
- Network Configuration: Ensure your firewall settings allow the necessary traffic.
- Resource Allocation: Monitor resource utilization to ensure proper allocation.

Conclusion

You have now set up a private cloud infrastructure using Eucalyptus. This "Cloud-in-a-Box" configuration allows you to manage and deploy virtual machines efficiently. Regularly monitor your cloud environment to ensure optimal performance and scalability.

Author Details

Dr. Rahul Sharma, working as Assistant Professor in Department of Computer Science and Engineering at Parul Institute of Technology, Parul University Vadodara, Gujarat. Prior to that he has more than + years of teaching experience in several engineering colleges as Chameli Devi Group of Institution, Indore and Dr. A.P.J. Abdul Kalam University, he completed B.E. (CSE) from Patel College of Science and Technology, Indore (M.P.) and M.Tech (NM&IS) from SCSIT, DAVV, Indore (M.P.). And PhD degree in Computer Science and Engineering from Rabindranath Tagore University Bhopal (M.P.). His research includes Computer Network, Network Security, Cryptography, Data Mining and Web Programming. He has 30+ research publications in reputed International journals, International- National conferences and 6 - patents (2 published- 4 Registered). He also qualified GATE (CSE) in 2015. He is publishing more than 16+ books in the field of computer science and Engineering.

Dr. Rishikesh Rawat Working as a Director in the Bansal College of Engineering. With his uttermost 21 years of experience in the field of engineering as a teacher and an administrator, has published several research papers in journals of international repute. He is the epitome of true excellence and has an interest lying in innovation, teaching, and learning pedagogy. He is also life member CSI & ISTEEnter Caption.

Mr. Deepak Kumar Khare is pursuing a Ph.D. in Computer Applications at Maulana Azad National Institute of Technology, Bhopal, M.P., India. Previously, he served as an Assistant Professor at the Institute of Engineering Technology, Dr. Rammanohar Lohiya Avadh University, Ayodhya, U.P., India, from September 2018 to September 2021. He also held the position of Assistant Professor at Radharaman Institute of Technology and Science, Bhopal, M.P., India, from December 2012 to August 2018. Mr. Khare earned his Master of Technology (M.Tech in Information Systems) from Maulana Azad National Institute of Technology, Bhopal, M.P., India, in 2010 and completed his Bachelor of Engineering (B.E. in Information Technology) at Rajiv Gandhi Proudyogiki Vishwavidyalaya, Bhopal, M.P., India, in 2008.

Dr. Vinod Patidar presently working as an Associate Professor in the Computer Science and Engineering department at Parul Institute of Technology (PIT), Parul University, Vadodara Gujarat, India. He has 16 years of experience.Earlier, He has served as an Assistant Professor at Bansal College of Engineering, Mandideep, Bhopal. He had been associated as an Assistant Professor at Scope College of Engineering, Bhopal (M.P.).He has completed his Doctor of Philosophy (Ph.D.) in the Topic of "Multi–Objective Virtual Machine Resource Allocation by Dynamic Load Scheduling Techniques", From Rabindranath Tagore University, Bhopal, (M.P.) In July, 2021. He has done Master of Technology (M. Tech) in CSE from University Institute of Technology (BU), Bhopal in 2013 and Bachelor of Engineering in CSE from University Institute of Technology (BU), Bhopal in 2006. Dr. Patidar is also a seasoned researcher with multiple publications in international journals, contributing valuable insights in areas such as artificial intelligence, Machine Learning, big data analytics, and dynamic load balancing.